# Great American One-Act Plays

Murray Schisgal
Thornton Wilder
Tennessee Williams
Edward Albee

Edited by
Stephen W. Souris

Ernst Klett Sprachen
Stuttgart

**Acknowledgments**

Murray Schisgal, *The Pushcart Peddlers*, copyright © 1981 by Murray Schisgal, from *The Best Short Plays* 1981 and Tennessee Williams, *The Last of My Solid Gold Watches*, copyright © 1945, 1953, 1981 by Tennessee Williams, from *The Theatre of Tennessee Williams*, Vol. 6 (1981) are reprinted by permission of International Creative Management, Inc., New York.

Edward Albee, *The Zoo Story*, copyright © 1959 by Edward Albee, is reprinted by permission of Stefani Hunzinger Bühnenverlag GmbH, Bad Homburg.

Thornton Wilder, *The Happy Journey to Trenton and Camden*, copyright © Thornton Wilder, 1959, from *The Long Christmas Dinner and Other Plays in One Act* (1931), is reprinted by permission of Paul und Peter Fritz AG, Zürich, acting on behalf of The Estate of Thornton Wilder.

1. Auflage        1     17 16 15 14  | 2028  27  26  25  24

Alle Drucke dieser Auflage sind unverändert und können im Unterricht nebeneinander benutzt werden. Die letzte Zahl bezeichnet das Jahr des Druckes.

www.klett-sprachen.de

Umschlagfoto: Shutterstock images / © Yellowj
Umschlaggestaltung: Elmar Feuerbach
Druck und Bindung: Digitaldruck Tebben GmbH, Biessenhofen

Printed in Germany.
ISBN 978-3-12-578218-1

# Contents

Preface . . . . . . . . . . . . . . . . . . . . . . . . . . . . . . . . . . . . . .   4

Murray Schisgal *The Pushcart Peddlers* . . . . . . . . . . . . . . . . . . .   5
Biographical Notes and Annotations . . . . . . . . . . . . . . . . . . . . . .  22

Thornton Wilder *The Happy Journey to Trenton and Camden* . . . . . .  26
Biographical Notes and Annotations . . . . . . . . . . . . . . . . . . . . . .  40

Tennessee Williams *The Last of My Solid Gold Watches* . . . . . . . . . .  43
Biographical Notes and Annotations . . . . . . . . . . . . . . . . . . . . . .  51

Edward Albee *The Zoo Story* . . . . . . . . . . . . . . . . . . . . . . . . . .  54
Biographical Notes and Annotations . . . . . . . . . . . . . . . . . . . . . .  74

# Preface

This collection of one-act plays deals with many aspects of American life. At the core, however, the plays are concerned with the whole range of the American experience: From the hope of the immigrants in Schisgal's *The Pushcart Peddlers* to despair in Albee's *The Zoo Story*.

The phonetic transcription in the *Annotations* is from D. Jones – A. C. Gimson, *Everyman's English Pronouncing Dictionary*, 14th edition.
The following abbreviations are used in the *Annotations:*

| | | | |
|---|---|---|---|
| *A.E.* | American English | *o.s.* | oneself |
| *B.E.* | British English | *s.b.* | somebody |
| *coll.* | colloquial | *s.o.* | someone |
| *sl.* | slang | *s.th.* | something |
| *dial.* | dialect | | |

Numbers in bold-face type in the margin refer to the corresponding pages in the text, those in light-face type to the lines of the respective page. Example: **25** 23 = page 25, line 23.

Murray Schisgal

# The Pushcart Peddlers

Characters:

CORNELIUS J. HOLLINGSWORTH III
SHIMMEL SHITZMAN
MAGGIE CUTWELL

5 Scene:
*Waterfront, New York City.*

Time:
*Many years ago.*

At Rise:
10 *A backdrop on which there is painted almost photographic, a symmetri-
cally designed Customs House, side and front view: smaller buildings
nearby.*
*Several kegs and wooden crates at both sides of backdrop. Lidded trash-
can, downstage.*
15 *Sound: waterfront noises, steamship whistle.*
*Music: in the style of the Ragtime section of Zukerman/Bolling "Suite for
Violin and Jazz Piano."*
*Cornelius, in vest, collarless shirt, baggy pants and a soiled derby, is seated
on a wooden box beside his banana-filled pushcart; his legs are crossed
20 and a newspaper is spread in front of his face.*
*Shimmel enters, looks about, and proceeds across stage. He carries a
battered suitcase, wears a threadbare suit, open-necked shirt and wilted tie,
a soft cap on his head.*
*Music out.*

25 CORNELIUS *(as Shimmel passes, peeks out from behind newspaper)*
Bananas. *(Shimmel stops, turns to Cornelius, waits in vain for him to
speak further, then moves on. Cornelius, peeking out from behind newspaper)* Bananas.
SHIMMEL *(stops again)* Excuse me.
30 CORNELIUS *(rises; folds and puts newspaper on pushcart; expansively)*
What a day! What a beautiful day. When I got up this morning I said to

myself, "This is going to be one rotten day." But look at it. Look for yourself. It's a beautiful day. Absolutely beautiful. It just goes to show you. You can't be too smart in this world. *(snaps open paper bag)* How many?

5 SHIMMEL  How many what?

CORNELIUS  How many bananas do you want?

SHIMMEL  I don't want any bananas.

CORNELIUS  You don't want any bananas?

SHIMMEL *(shakes his head)*  No.

10 CORNELIUS  Then why did you disturb me?

SHIMMEL  I thought you were talking to me.

CORNELIUS  You thought ...? Why should I talk to you? Are you a millionaire? *(Shimmel shakes his head.)* Are you a politician? *(Shimmel shakes his head.)* Are you a celebrity? *(Shimmel shakes his head.)*
15 Then why should I talk to you?

SHIMMEL  I ... I'm sorry, I made a mistake. It is a beautiful day. A wonderful day. Excuse me. *(He starts off.)*

CORNELIUS *(returns paper bag)*  The nerve of some people. Coming over and making a spectacle of themselves. Hey, you!

20 SHIMMEL *(runs to him)*  Yes?

CORNELIUS  Who are you, anyway?

SHIMMEL *(removes cap, pushes it into jacket pocket)*  Shitzman. Shimmel Shitzman.

CORNELIUS *(amazed)*  You're Shimmel Shitzman?

25 SHIMMEL  Do you know me?

CORNELIUS  Why should I know you? Are you a millionaire? *(Shimmel shakes his head.)* Are you a politician? *(Shimmel shakes his head.)* Are you a celebrity? *(Shimmel shakes his head.)* Then why should I know you?

30 SHIMMEL  I thought you ...

CORNELIUS  Where are you from, Shimmel Shitzman?

SHIMMEL  From the vicinity of Kovno-Vilna.

CORNELIUS *(amazed)*  You're from the vicinity of Kovno-Vilna?

SHIMMEL  Are you from the vicinity of Kovno-Vilna?

35 CORNELIUS *(dusts bananas with feather mop)*  As a matter of fact, I'm not. I'm from the vicinity of Minsk-Pinsk.

SHIMMEL *(enthusiastically)*  Minsk-Pinsk! Why, that's practically walking distance from the vicinity of Kovno-Vilna. We're practically neighbors!

CORNELIUS  Does that surprise you?

40 SHIMMEL  In all honesty, it does. You're the first person I talked to since I

got off the boat. And to talk to someone who was practically my neighbor in the old country, that's what I call a stroke of good luck. Can I ask you a few impersonal questions, neighbor?

CORNELIUS *(sits)* So long as you don't take up too much of my time, neighbor. You happen to have caught me during my rush hour.

SHIMMEL Business is good?

CORNELIUS Business is excellent. Couldn't be better.

SHIMMEL When did you arrive from Minsk-Pinsk?

CORNELIUS Is today Tuesday or Wednesday?

SHIMMEL Wednesday.

CORNELIUS Then I arrived yesterday.

SHIMMEL *(puts suitcase down)* You arrived yesterday from Minsk-Pinsk?

CORNELIUS That's correct.

SHIMMEL And you're in business for yourself already?

CORNELIUS That's correct. *(He lights a cigar butt.)*

SHIMMEL Why, that's wonderful, marvelous!

CORNELIUS You think that's wonderful, marvelous? I heard of a man from the vicinity of Ozrokow-Pruszkow who arrived here in the morning and owned two factories, three warehouses and a hotel in the Catskill Mountains before he sat down for lunch!

SHIMMEL Fantastic! What a country this is! What a great country. I can't wait to get started myself, but ...

CORNELIUS But what?

SHIMMEL I don't know where to begin.

CORNELIUS Well, since we're practically from the same vicinity ... maybe I can give you a hint or two.

SHIMMEL *(sits on suitcase)* I would appreciate that more than anything in the world.

CORNELIUS *(with emphasis)* Are you listening?

SHIMMEL I'm listening.

CORNELIUS Are you paying attention?

SHIMMEL I'm paying attention.

CORNELIUS First thing you have to do ...

SHIMMEL Yes?

CORNELIUS Is buy yourself an American name.

SHIMMEL Buy myself an American name?

CORNELIUS That's absolutely essential, *(steps on cigar butt; takes slips of papers from vest pocket.)* And I'll tell you something else, neighbor: this is your lucky day. It so happens I have several American names that are up for sale.

SHIMMEL  But what's wrong with Shimmel Shitzman?

CORNELIUS  Shimmel Shitzman? They'll laugh you out of the country with a name like that. Do you know what my name was when I got off the boat? *(Shimmel shakes his head.)* Elias Crapavarnishkes.

5 SHIMMEL  Crapavarnishkes. That's not a bad name. There was a judge from the vicinity of Lvov who had the name Crapavarnishkes. He was a very respected man.

CORNELIUS  Your Judge Crapavarnishkes couldn't get a job as a street cleaner here. The first thing I did when I got off the boat was to buy

10 myself a brand new legitimate name. And since then I've been prospering beyond my wildest dreams.

SHIMMEL  That's fantastic. What is your American name?

CORNELIUS *(slight English accent)*  Cornelius J. Hollingsworth.

SHIMMEL  Wow!

15 CORNELIUS  The Third.

SHIMMEL  The Third?

CORNELIUS  That's correct. It cost me fifteen dollars with the middle initial and the Third thrown in. It was the only one like it they had. I could have gotten John Smith for fifty cents, but I wouldn't have any part of it. Well,

20 what do you say, Mr. Shitzman? *(Reading from slips of paper.)* I have Andrew Hamilton for five dollars, Sylvester Peterson for six-fifty, Thomas Hathaway, six dollars and fifteen cents, Roger Williams Carnegie, five seventy-five, Samuel P. Stone, five dollars without the tax ...

SHIMMEL  I'm sorry, Mr. Hollingsworth. I couldn't change my name. It's

25 been in my family for generations. I was born a Shitzman and I guess I'll have to die a Shitzman.

CORNELIUS *(returning slips of paper to vest pocket)*  Have it your own way. But don't say I didn't try to help you. It just goes to show: mind your own business and you're better off. *(Indignantly, he spreads newspaper in*

30 *front of his face.)*

SHIMMEL *(rises; lifts suitcase)*  Mr. Hollingsworth?

CORNELIUS *(behind newspaper)*  What is it now?

SHIMMEL  Can I ask you one more question?

CORNELIUS *(behind newspaper)*  I told you I was busy! I don't have all day

35 to sit here and chat with you!

SHIMMEL  One more question and I won't bother you any more, I promise.

CORNELIUS *(puts newspaper aside)*  Go on. What is it? What is it?

SHIMMEL *(puts suitcase down)*  Where do you think I should look for a job?

CORNELIUS  A job? Why do you want to look for a job?

40 SHIMMEL  To work. To earn money ...

CORNELIUS   Ridiculous. Nobody comes to this country to look for a job. There's no future in it. You have to go into business for yourself. It's the only decent way to make a living here.

SHIMMEL *(sits on suitcase)*   But I don't know anything about going into
5   business. I'm a worker. I have experience as a tinsmith, a carpenter, a ...

CORNELIUS   You people from the vicinity of Kovno-Vilna are all a bunch of blockheads! What did I know about going into business when I got off the boat? Nothing. Absolutely nothing. I was a shoemaker, a leather-stitcher. But did I let that stop me? Not on your life. I used my head and
10   here I am: in business for myself!

SHIMMEL   But what kind of business could I get into? I don't have much capital ...

CORNELIUS   Ohhh, there are plenty of good profitable businesses you can go into. Why don't you open your eyes and look around and see what's
15   available? *(As Shimmel rises and "looks around," Cornelius plants a FOR SALE on his pushcart.)*  If I were you, Mr. Shitzman, I'd grab the first business up for sale and get right to work. I wouldn't waste any time. Things happen fast in this country. Very fast. You have to stay up on your toes and use your old noodle! *(He spreads newspaper in front of his*
20   *face.)*

SHIMMEL *(turns to see sign on pushcart)*   Mr. Hollingsworth?

CORNELIUS *(behind newspaper)*   Yes?

SHIMMEL   Is your ... business up for sale?

CORNELIUS *(folds newspaper; stares at FOR SALE sign)*   Hmmmmmm. As
25   a matter of fact, it is.

SHIMMEL   Do you think I could make a go of it?

CORNELIUS *(puts newspaper aside; rises)*   You?

SHIMMEL *(nods)*   Me.

CORNELIUS   Hmmmmmm. That's a *tough* question. Let me hear you say:
30   bananas.

SHIMMEL   Bananas.

CORNELIUS   Hmmmmmm. You're not without talent. Let me hear you say: bananas, bananas, get your fresh ripe bananas!

SHIMMEL   Bananas, bananas, get your fresh ripe bananas!

35 CORNELIUS   Try it a little louder and try to speak out of the side of your mouth so your voice has a distinctive quality: bananas, bananas, get your fresh ripe bananas!

SHIMMEL *(imitating him: from the side of his mouth, jerking his head)*   Bananas, bananas, get your fresh ripe bananas!

40 CORNELIUS   No, no, your arms have to swing out, from the side, as if you

own the whole street. And kick your leg up a little. Like this.   *(demonstrating: throws arms out, kicks up one leg, tips derby on last word)* Bananas, bananas, get your fresh ripe bananas! *(to Shimmel)* Try it. *(He puts derby on Shimmel's head; sits on trash can.)*

5   SHIMMEL *(imitating him)*   Bananas, bananas, get your fresh ripe bananas! *(tips derby)*

CORNELIUS   Excellent. Excellent. How did it feel?

SHIMMEL   Fine. It felt fine.

CORNELIUS   Were you relaxed? Were you comfortable?

10   SHIMMEL   I was very relaxed and comfortable.

CORNELIUS *(rises)*   I'm going to tell you something now, Mr. Shitzman: between the two of us and the pushcart, you'll make a fortune in this business.

SHIMMEL *(excitedly)*   You think so?

15   CORNELIUS *(takes derby from Shimmel's head; puts it on)*   I know so. It's a definite positive.

SHIMMEL   How much would it cost me?

CORNELIUS *(moves to pushcart; arms outspread)*   The whooole business?

SHIMMEL *(nods)*   The whole business.

20   CORNELIUS   Hmmmmmm. I could ... no, no, I couldn't do that. We're practically from the same vicinity. Let me ask you this, Mr. Shitzman. How much do you have?

SHIMMEL   I have exactly ... *(takes out change purse)*   Forty-three dollars and twenty-five cents.

25   CORNELIUS   Could you raise another six dollars and seventy-five cents by five o'clock?

SHIMMEL *(sits on trash can)*   How? I don't know anyone here.

CORNELIUS *(sits on box)*   What a shame! I couldn't possibly sell for under fifty dollars unless ... *(rises)*

30   SHIMMEL *(rises)*   Unless what?

CORNELIUS   Unless I took a bunch of bananas to make up the difference.

SHIMMEL   A bunch of bananas is worth six dollars and seventy-five cents?

CORNELIUS *(He picks up a bunch of bananas.)*   Are you serious? Do you
35   know what they call a bunch of bananas in this country? *(Shimmel shakes his head. Cornelius holds out bananas, pointed upwards.)* Goldfingers.

SHIMMEL   That's fantastic! Here you are, Mr. Hollingsworth. *(gives him money)*   I'm anxious to get right to work. Do I need any papers to prove
40   ownership?

CORNELIUS *(bananas under arm)* You'll find them under the fifth banana in the fourth row from the left. *(shakes his hand)* Congratulations Mr. Shitzman. And the best of everything to you.

SHIMMEL Thank you. Thank you, Mr. Hollingsworth.

5 CORNELIUS *(moving off)* I have to be off now. If you sell out, go to Pier 26 and ask for Pete. He'll give you a fair shake.

SHIMMEL *(shouts after him)* Thanks again, Mr. Hollingsworth. And drop around and say hello once in a while! *(Music. Shimmel puts on cap, carries suitcase behind pushcart, places FOR SALE sign on top of it; he*
10 *then examines pushcart, proudly, with proprietary air; he dusts off bananas with feather mop, dusts off his jacket, looks about as if he owns the whole street. He suddenly shouts, swinging his arms, kicks up a leg, in imitation of Cornelius.)* Bananas, bananas, get your fresh ripe bananas! *(He runs to pushcart, snaps open a paper bag, as if expecting an avalanche*
15 *of customers. Undismayed he returns paper bag, sits on box, crossing his legs, and spreads the newspaper in front of his face. Offstage Cornelius shouts, "Bananas, bananas, get your fresh ripe bananas!" Shimmel lowers his newspaper and gapes in astonishment as Cornelius rolls in a second pushcart, an exact replica of the one he sold to him, shouting, two or three*
20 *times more, "Bananas, bananas, get your fresh ripe bananas!" Cornelius stops his pushcart parallel to Shimmel's, removes a wooden box from it, sits down and unfolds a newspaper in front of his face. Music out. Shimmel removes his cap, speaks softly, uncertainly.)* Mr. Hollingsworth?

CORNELIUS *(behind newspaper)* Yes?

25 SHIMMEL You're not staying here, are you?

CORNELIUS *(behind newspaper)* Of course I'm staying here. *(reads aloud)* Hmmmmmm. This is interesting. "Bride hurls wedding cake at groom for criticizing her dress. Brawl ensues." *(He hawks a laugh.)*

SHIMMEL But ...

30 CORNELIUS But what?

SHIMMEL But can we both make a living selling the same merchandise at the same location?

CORNELIUS *(puts newspaper aside; rises)* Unfortunately we can't. The competition will force us to lower the price and we'll probably have to begin
35 bankruptcy proceedings in a matter of days. *(shouts)* Bananas, bananas!

SHIMMEL *(rises; desperately)* Mr. Hollingsworth!

CORNELIUS What is it now?

SHIMMEL I don't want to sound rude, but if we both can't make a living
40 here, why don't you be considerate and go somewhere else?

CORNELIUS  Why don't I ... *(sharply)* Why don't you be considerate and go somewhere else?

SHIMMEL  It was my understanding when you sold me this business that I would be the only one at this location. Otherwise I can assure you, I would have thought twice about buying it!

CORNELIUS  Ohhh, it was your understanding! But I didn't say anything to that effect, did I?

SHIMMEL  You didn't have to ...

CORNELIUS  This is a free country, Mr. Shitzman, and I have as much right to sell at this location as you have! *(shouts)* Bananas, bananas!

SHIMMEL  Can't we talk about it? *(shouts in a panic)* Bananas, bananas!

CORNELIUS  Talk, who's stopping you? *(shouts)* Bananas, bananas!

SHIMMEL  I'm new here, Mr. Hollingsworth. I don't know this city! *(shouts)* Bananas, bananas!

CORNELIUS  Mr. Shitzman, I have to make a living, too. My customers expect to find me here and I'm not disappointing them! Not for you or the King of Siam! *(shouts)* Bananas, bananas!

SHIMMEL  Mr. Hollingsworth, I gave you my last penny! I trusted you! *(shouts)* Bananas, bananas!

CORNELIUS  I can't help you more than I did, Mr. Shitzman! *(shouts)* Bananas! Bana ... *(Suddenly turns to Shimmel.)* Unless ...

SHIMMEL *(eagerly)*  Unless what?

CORNELIUS  Unless we went into partnership.

SHIMMEL  Partnership?

CORNELIUS *(nods)*  The two of us.

SHIMMEL  Why, that would be wonderful, Mr. ...

CORNELIUS *(grins)*  Call me Cornelius.

SHIMMEL  Cornelius. Cornelius, that would be wonderful! It would solve all our problems! We could work together, cooperate ...

CORNELIUS  There's only one thing that stands in the way.

SHIMMEL  What's that?

CORNELIUS *(sits on trash can)*  Money.

SHIMMEL  Money?

CORNELIUS  That's correct. Money. You don't expect us to become full and equal partners with all my experience, do you?

SHIMMEL  But I don't have any money left, Mr. ... Cornelius. I gave you my last penny, word of honor. *(He raises his hand.)*

CORNELIUS  Can't you borrow some from friends or relatives or a philanthropic organization?

SHIMMEL *(sits on box)*  Impossible. I told you, I don't know anyone here.

CORNELIUS *(rises)* Then there's only one thing for us to do.

SHIMMEL *(rises)* What's that?

CORNELIUS Negotiate.

SHIMMEL Can we negotiate without money?

5 CORNELIUS Of course.

SHIMMEL How do we do it?

CORNELIUS *(using his hands)* It's simple. You make an offer. I refuse your offer and make a counter-offer. You refuse my counter-offer and make a counter-counter-offer of your own. I refuse your counter-counter-offer

10 and I make what is called a proposal which leads you to make a counter-proposal and so on and so forth and so on and so forth until we whittle the difference to nil and come to equitable terms.

SHIMMEL But I still don't have any money.

CORNELIUS Who's talking about money! Jesus Christ, you are a dumb-

15 dumb. We negotiate percentages! *(Throws arms out at one pushcart, then the other.)* How much of the business do you own in contradistinction to how much of the business do I own! *(He sits on box, crosses legs, puts newspaper in front of his face.)* Make me an offer.

SHIMMEL On a percentage of the business?

20 CORNELIUS *(behind newspaper)* That's correct. Do it formally.

SHIMMEL Yes, sir. *(Puts on cap, brushes jacket; clears throat.)* Excuse me, Mr. Hollingsworth.

CORNELIUS *(newspaper on lap; innocently)* Did you wish to speak to me, sir?

25 SHIMMEL Yes, sir. About the possibility of our going into partnership, sir. I make an offer that you receive fifty percent of the business and I receive fifty percent of the business ... sir.

CORNELIUS What about my superior experience, sir?

SHIMMEL I can learn the business very quickly and if I work twice as hard

30 that will offset the difference, sir.

CORNELIUS No deal, sir. I respectfully decline your offer. *(Newspaper in front of his face.)*

SHIMMEL *(clears throat; whispers)* You make your counter-offer now. *(no response)* I make my offer, fifty-fifty, you're supposed to make a

35 counter-offer. *(no response; loudly)* Aren't you going to make me a counter-offer, sir? Did I do anything improper, sir? *(desperately)* Mr. Hollingsworth, we have to reach an agreement! You yourself said we both can't make a living here! For God's sake, make me a counter-offer!

CORNELIUS *(lowers newspaper)* Bananas, ripe lovely bananas here!

40 *(Newspaper in front of his face.)*

SHIMMEL   This is crazy! You're being unfair, unreasonable! I ... *(resigned to it)* All right, sixty-forty! Sixty for you, forty for me. Is it a deal sir?

CORNELIUS *(puts newspaper aside: shouts)* Bananas, get your ripe lovely bananas here! *(without looking at him; coaching him)* Get down on
5   your knees. Beg me. Tell me how hard up you are. Tell me your family depends on you for support. Get to me emotionally. *(shouts)* Bananas, bananas here! Get your ripe bananas!

SHIMMEL *(on his knees)* Mr. Hollingsworth, I beg you to consider my offer. I think it's very equitable. Besides, I'm broke. I don't have a
10   penny. I don't have money to buy dinner tonight ... I don't have a roof over my head ... *(Cornelius rises, paces. Shimmel is emotional indeed, on the verge of tears, building his lines to a crescendo.)* Mr. Hollingsworth, my family is still in the old country. They're depending on me to send them something each week. I have an elderly father who's confined
15   to his bed. My mother suffers from arthritis and bursitis. My two little sisters don't have clothes to wear to school. My baby brother, my little baby brother ... *(He breaks into sobs.)*

CORNELIUS *(tears streaming down his cheeks)* What a terrible story. What a tragedy. How old is your little baby brother?

20   SHIMMEL *(weeping)* Who knows? Who knows?

CORNELIUS *(weeping)* What dis-ease, what afflic-tion does he have?

SHIMMEL *(weeping; louder)* Who knows? Who knows?

CORNELIUS *(weeping)* Your two little sisters ...

SHIMMEL *(weeping; still louder)* My two little sisters ... without clothes!

25   CORNELIUS *(weeping)* Don't say another word, Shimmel. Please, please don't! Not another word! I'll help you. I'll do whatever you want.

SHIMMEL *(rises)* Does that mean we're partners?

CORNELIUS   Sixty-forty?

SHIMMEL *(nods)* Sixty-forty!

30   CORNELIUS *(embracing him)* Partner!

SHIMMEL   Thank you, Cornelius; thank you.

CORNELIUS *(breaks away, takes out handkerchief, blows his nose)* Oh, boy, that was a good cry. Oh, boy. I have to admit ... I enjoyed it thoroughly.

SHIMMEL *(wiping his eyes)* I did, too. I didn't know that negotiations could
35   be so emotional.

CORNELIUS   There's a lot you have to learn, partner. But don't worry. I'll teach you every aspect of this business. From now on your gain becomes under contract my profit. Okay, now let's get to work. No more horsing around.

*(Music. Cornelius sits down on box, crosses legs, spreads newspaper in front of his face. Shimmel, imitating him, does likewise. Cornelius soon rises, yawns, stretches his arms over his head, shakes out one leg, then the other, looks about, then flaps handkerchief over top of wooden box before*
5   *sitting down, spreading newspaper in front of his face. Shimmel does likewise, but before spreading newspaper in front of his face, speaks. Music out.)*

SHIMMEL   Cornelius?

CORNELIUS *(behind newspaper)*   Yes?

10  SHIMMEL   How's business?

CORNELIUS *(newspaper on lap)*   Excellent. Excellent. If it keeps up at this rate, I think we should buy another pushcart.

SHIMMEL   Can we afford it?

CORNELIUS   What a question.

15  SHIMMEL   I didn't know we were that successful.

CORNELIUS   If I told you how successful we were, Shimmel, you'd get a swollen head, so let's not discuss it and just keep working.

SHIMMEL   I will. I promise. You'll get nothing but hard work from me.

CORNELIUS   That's what I expect from you. Now let's get to work.

20  *(They both spread their newspapers in front of their faces. Romantic, lyrical music. Maggie Cutwell, a young, very pretty girl, in a shapeless black frock, enters, carrying a tray of small bunches of colorful flowers strapped around her neck. She walks with her hand held slightly in front of her.)*

25  MAGGIE *(in a sweet, angelic voice)*   Flowers. Flowers. Pretty flowers for sale. Fresh, pretty flowers. *(She doesn't turn to the men but stands at the side of Shimmel's pushcart, staring forward. She wipes her perspiring face with a rag. Music out.)*

SHIMMEL *(whispers; puts newspaper aside)*   Cornelius? Do you see that?

30  CORNELIUS *(puts newspaper aside)*   Oh, yes.

SHIMMEL   She's beautiful, isn't she?

CORNELIUS   I've seen better heads on cabbages. But it's a pity, just the same.

SHIMMEL   What's a pity?

35  CORNELIUS   She's blind.

SHIMMEL   Is she?

CORNELIUS   All the flower girls are blind in this country.

SHIMMEL   That is a pity. She looks destitute. She looks like she hasn't had a piece of food in her mouth all day. Cornelius, can I get a credit for one banana?

CORNELIUS *(makes an entry in notebook)*   If you want to be extravagant . . .

SHIMMEL   Thank you.   *(He takes banana from pushcart and moves to Maggie. She doesn't turn to look at him. Gently he places the banana on her flower tray; returns to his seat.)*

MAGGIE *(looks down at banana; shouts)*   Get your fucking banana off my fucking flowers!

SHIMMEL *(jumps up, retrieves banana)*   Forgive me. I . . . I thought you were blind.

MAGGIE   I'll give you blind in a minute. I'll poke out both your eyes and feed 'em to the cats!

SHIMMEL   But I . . .

MAGGIE   I know what you're after, Buster! If I wanted to be a whore, I wouldn't be selling these fucking flowers!

SHIMMEL   You're mistaken, believe me. I only wanted to help you.

MAGGIE   Yeah, and how the hell were you gonna do that? By slipping me a banana?

SHIMMEL   I thought you were hungry.

MAGGIE   I don't need your lousy banana. If I'm hungry, I know where to eat. I've been taking care of myself since I'm six years old and I haven't starved to death yet!

SHIMMEL   You're an orphan?

MAGGIE   You bet your sweet ass!

SHIMMEL   I'm sorry. Life must have been difficult for you.

MAGGIE   I got no complaints. How about buying a bunch of these stink-weeds for your girl friend?

SHIMMEL   I'm afraid I have no money. *(laughs self-consciously)* I have no girl friend either.

MAGGIE   That figures, you crumb-bum, you creep! Wasting a girl's time for nothing. I oughta call the police. I oughta bop you in the nose. *(Shouts as she forces him back so that he sits on trash can.)* Get away from me! I hate your lousy guts! *(Suddenly in a sweet, angelic voice.)* Flowers. Pretty flowers for sale. Fresh pretty flowers. *(Cornelius rises, derby in hand; he moves to Maggie, speaks with great formality.)*

CORNELIUS   Allow me to apologize for my partner, ma'am. He's new here. He has no sense of propriety.

MAGGIE   They should send him back where he came from, the creep! Doesn't he have the decency to introduce himself like a gentleman? Did his parents name him before they dumped him into a garbage can?

CORNELIUS His name is Shitzman. Shimmel Shitzman.

*(Shimmel stands as if expecting an introduction.)*

MAGGIE Shitzman! Shimmel Shitzman! *(She breaks out into laughter.)* It
fits him. It fits him perfectly. *(to Shimmel)* Shitzman. Mr. Shitzman!
5 *(And she laughs again.)*

*(Shimmel sits down on trash can, dejectedly.)*

CORNELIUS *(bows)* Perhaps you'd be good enough to permit me to introduce myself to you, ma'am. I am Cornelius J. Hollingsworth, the Third.

MAGGIE *(curtsies a bit)* Pleased to make your acquaintance, Mr.
10 Hollingsworth. I am Maggie Cutwell and although I find it necessary to
sell flowers in order to sustain myself, I am by profession an actress, a
thespian, a tap dancer, a toe dancer, and a highly regarded chanteuse.

CORNELIUS All good fortune to you, Miss Cutwell. I am myself in the
banana business at present, but it is merely transitional. My one true and
15 genuine ambition is to gain a seat on the Stock Exchange and invest
substantial sums of money in musical comedy productions. *(Puts on
derby.)*

MAGGIE Am I to believe that it is your intention to become a theatrical
producer?

20 CORNELIUS Precisely, Miss Cutwell. *(picks up a banana)* May I offer you
a banana?

MAGGIE *(takes it from him)* I will be happy to take your banana, Mr.
Hollingsworth, but I will never take his banana. *(to Shimmel)* Never!
Not even if it was covered with diamonds!

25 CORNELIUS I am doing all I can for him, Miss Cutwell, but it's a sad, a
terribly sad and tragic story.

MAGGIE I'm sure it is.

CORNELIUS How much are your flowers, Miss Cutwell?

MAGGIE These are ten cents a bunch, and those wilted ones on the side are
30 three cents a bunch.

CORNELIUS I would like to purchase two ten cent bunches, please. *(She
hands them to him; he gives her the coins.)* Thank you. Here's your
money and these ... these are for you. *(Gallantly he hands her back the
flowers. He then passes Shimmel, extending his arms as if to say, "See how
35 easy it is?")*

MAGGIE You are a very kind person, I can see that right away. Mr.
Hollingsworth, it may be premature of me to suggest, but in the event
you actually become a theatrical producer in the foreseeable future,

could you possibly keep me in mind for a part in one of your musical productions?

CORNELIUS  To be frank with you, Miss Cutwell, I don't know whether you're talented or not.

5  MAGGIE  Can't I show you? Won't you at least give me the opportunity to show you what I can do?

CORNELIUS  Ordinarily I would say yes immediately, without reservation, but you've caught me during my busiest day of the week. It's impossible. I can't. I have obligations. *(He puts foot on box, ties his shoelace.)*

10  MAGGIE  Please, Mr. Hollingsworth! This is extremely important to me. If I don't succeed in my chosen profession, I'll have to go on selling flowers for the rest of my life, or marry some beer-bellied creep who'd beat me every night just for the exercise. I'll be forced to kill myself, Mr. Hollingsworth! *(Cornelius turns to her as she gets down on her knees.)*

15  I couldn't go on living like that, I couldn't, I couldn't ... *(She weeps.)*

CORNELIUS  *(tears streaming down his cheeks)*  What a tragedy. What a terrible, terrible story. How long have you been selling flowers?

MAGGIE  *(weeping)*  Ever since I was six years old.

CORNELIUS  *(weeping)*  Tragic. Tragic. Have you experienced no pleasure,
20  no happiness, no joy in all your young years?

MAGGIE  *(weeping)*  No. Nothing but pain and heartache.

CORNELIUS  *(weeping)*  Ohhhhh, pain and heartache. And you would take your own life?

MAGGIE  *(weeping)*  Yes, yes, I have the pills at home and today there was a
25  sale at Woolworth's and I bought ... I bought six bottles of iodine!

CORNELIUS  *(moves away; she follows him on her knees)*  No more, Miss Cutwell. No more. I can't take it. I can't. It's too much for a human being to bear. If you'd like to perform for me, go home, change, rearrange your appearance, prepare yourself, and come back when you're ready. But
30  please, hurry. I don't have the time! I have a business to run here!

MAGGIE  Thank you. Thank you. You're my light in the darkness. You're my savior. *(rises)*  Two minutes, Mr. Hollingsworth. *(turns to Shimmel)*  Two minutes ... Sh-Sh-Sh-Sh-Shitzman? Shitzman? That's a riot. Shitzman. *(And she exits.)*

35  CORNELIUS  *(sits on box)*  Well, what do you think?

SHIMMEL  *(rises; looks after Maggie)*  I ... I think she's beautiful.

CORNELIUS  Good. I'm glad you feel that way because I'd like you to get her off my hands.

SHIMMEL  But I thought ...

40  CORNELIUS  *(rises; moves to him)*  Don't think, Shimmel. You can be

arrested for it. Feel, feel, start feeling and start expressing your feelings, your fantasies, your dreams! Use your imagination! You're a very repressed person. If I had known that before, I would never have gone into partnership with you!

5 SHIMMEL But why do you want me to take Miss Cutwell off your hands? Aren't you attracted to her?

CORNELIUS Attracted, retracted, contracted, who has time for those shenanigans. It so happens, be it as it may, willy-nilly, hocus-pocus, I'm a married man. *(moves toward his box; stops)* I also have three brats.

10 *(moves; stops)* And a gypsy girl friend. *(moves)* It's unprofessional for me to get further involved. *(Sits on box.)*

SHIMMEL I'd be very glad to take her off your hands.

CORNELIUS Excellent. Excellent. *(rises)* Unfortunately one problem remains.

15 SHIMMEL What's that?

CORNELIUS Our partnership name. Hollingsworth and Shitzman. It's out of the question. Didn't you hear how Miss Cutwell laughed at it? We'll get the same treatment from everyone who hears it. We'll be the laughing stock of the banana business.

20 SHIMMEL But I told you ...

CORNELIUS *(shouts)* I know what you told me! I know what you said! But don't I count for anything? Shimmel, please! Consider someone else for a change? There's no limit to how far we could go together, but you're destroying everything we created with your ridiculous name! It's like a

25 cancer preventing our full growth and prosperity!

SHIMMEL Even if I wanted to ... I don't have the money ...

CORNELIUS *(sits on box)* We'll negotiate. I'll take an I.O.U. I'll place a lien on your forty percent. Don't worry about it. *(pulls out slips of paper)* Now what will it be? Thomas Hathaway. Roger Williams Carnegie.

30 Samuel P. Stone ...

SHIMMEL *(pleading)* Cornelius, my family name ... *(sits on box)*

CORNELIUS Which one, Shimmel? Which one? *(Shimmel doesn't reply. Cornelius rises; hands him slip of paper.)* Samuel P. Stone it is! Five dollars even. Hollingsworth and Stone. Perfect. It couldn't be better.

35 Congratulations, partner. *(sits; makes entry in notebook)* Well, do you feel any differently, Sam? *(Shimmel shakes his head.)* You have to feel differently. A Crapavarnishkes isn't a Hollingsworth and a Shitzman isn't a Stone.

SHIMMEL Samuel P. Stone. I am Samuel P. Stone.

40 CORNELIUS Sam Stone!

SHIMMEL *(rises)*   I am Sam Stone. *(He faces upstage.)*

CORNELIUS   That's it. Feel Stone. Feel rock. Feel hard. Feel firm. Feel strong. Feel ...

*(Maggie rushes back in, wearing a Shirley Temple dress and tap shoes.)*

5   MAGGIE *(panting)*   I'm here, Mr. Hollingsworth! I'm ready to perform for you.

CORNELIUS *(rises)*   Yes, yes, but before you begin, I'd like to introduce you to my partner, Sam Stone.

MAGGIE   But that's Mr. Shitzman. I met him ...

10   CORNELIUS   I beg to differ with you, Miss Cutwell. That *was* Mr. Shitzman. But he has changed considerably since you last saw him.

*(Shimmel turns downstage, posture straight, hand in pocket; speaks with pronounced certainty and sophistication.)*

SHIMMEL   That's correct, Miss Cutwell. And if you've come to perform for
15   us, please begin. We don't have all day to dilly-dally.

*(Both men nod to each other, curtly, and return to sit on their boxes. Maggie looks about to make sure no one is about, then breaks into a bright song and tap dance, something in the style of "I Don't Care." She sings intro without moving, merely bouncing up and down, hands clenched as if
20   riding a horse. She tap dances as she sings the chorus, moving around the peddlers, posing beside them – a nightclub performance of sorts. This is followed by a tap dance as she da-da's tune of chorus. She ends by whirling around several times, almost stumbling. Her talent is not noteworthy. When she is done, she turns to them, waits breathlessly for their verdict.)*

25   CORNELIUS   Sam?

SHIMMEL   Yes, Cornelius?

CORNELIUS   What do you think of her performance?

SHIMMEL *(rises; fervently)*   What do I think? Do you have to ask? Are you blind? Are you deaf? Do you not have a heart to feel with? I have just
30   witnessed a performance of such precision, of such exquisiteness and beauty, that if I were in the producing business today, this young lady would be a star tomorrow!

MAGGIE *(embracing him)*   Oh, Mr. Stone! You don't know how much I needed to hear that! You made me so happy!

35   SHIMMEL *(circling around her)*   Enough of this, enough! You have a lot of work to do, Maggie. I am not now in the producing business, but I have every hope of being in the producing business in the very near future. Go

home and practice! Practice! Practice! Day and night! Twenty-four hours around the clock! I'm going to be relentless with you, I give you fair warning. I'll pay the bills; I'll see to it that you have the necessities ... *(stops circling; holds her chin in his hand)* But I want you to be the best

5   there is, the absolute best!

MAGGIE   I will be! I will! *(Starts off.)*

SHIMMEL   And Maggie ...

MAGGIE *(returns)*   Yes, Mr. Stone?

SHIMMEL   No intimacy. No personal relationship. This is strictly a profes-

10   sional deal, is that clear?

MAGGIE   Yes, Mr. Stone. *(Starts off.)*

SHIMMEL   Where did you say you lived?

MAGGIE *(returns)*   Number eleven Perry Street.

SHIMMEL   I'll be up this evening to formalize our contractual arrangement.

15 MAGGIE   I'll be home. I'll be practicing.

SHIMMEL   Have a bite for me to eat. I'll be hungry and tired.

MAGGIE   I'll put a tuna fish casserole in the oven. Thank you. Thank you, Mr. Stone. I have hope. You gave me hope. God bless you! *(She kisses him on cheek, runs off, singing a line or two of song ending with "2, 3, 4!")*

20 SHIMMEL *(staring after her)*   What a girl! What an incredible girl!

CORNELIUS   So you've become fond of her.

SHIMMEL   Fond of her? I'm in love with her! I'm head-over-heels in love with her! Cornelius, Cornelius, I never felt this way before. I never thought I could feel this way. My heart is in my mouth. I have a tempera-

25   ture of over a hundred. My legs are shaking. My stomach is bubbling. It's too much. I can't breathe. Is all this happening to me or am I dreaming? Did I meet someone named Maggie Cutwell or did I make it up? Pinch me, Cornelius, pinch me! I have to know the truth!

CORNELIUS *(rises)*   Hold it, Sam, just hold it a minute! I have to ask you:

30   are you rich enough to support yourself and her, too? After all, you just started in business, this is your first day here ... I don't unterstand. How can you ...

SHIMMEL   You don't understand! Of course you don't understand! You don't look, you don't listen, you don't pay attention! I met a woman I

35   love, Cornelius. I'm going to marry her. She is going to appear in a musical that I am going to produce ... *(points)* with you! Now I have the inspiration, the dedication to succeed in a big way. Nothing can stop me. Nothing! Now, come, no more horsing around. This is a matter of life and death to me. Let's get to work *(He sits on box, crosses legs, puts*

40 *newspaper in front of his face.)*

CORNELIUS *(stares at him, incredulously; then sits on box, takes news-paper)*   How's business, Sam?

SHIMMEL *(behind newspaper)*   Good, Cornelius. Excellent.

CORNELIUS   You know, I think it's time we started a corporation. What do
5   you think?

SHIMMEL *(newspaper down)*   I don't know why we waited so long.

CORNELIUS   If I have one fault, it's being too conservative.   *(Shimmel puts newspaper in front of his face.)*

CORNELIUS   Sam?

10   SHIMMEL *(newspaper down)*   Yes, Cornelius?

CORNELIUS *(simply)*   Welcome to America.   *(Music as they both lift news-papers in front of their faces, simultaneously uncross and cross their legs – left over right, then right over left – with music punctuating their actions and ending abruptly. Blackout)*

## Biographical Notes

*Murray Schisgal, the son of an immigrant from Vilna, Lithuania, was born in 1926. He has been a New Yorker since birth. He became a serious writer in his late teens, but it was about a decade before he became known.*

*Schisgal, who is a member of the American avant-garde, often takes as his subject the superficiality of modern civilization. He has managed to survive the rise and fall of absurdism by mocking the elements of self-love, self-pity and self-dramatization which often characterize the pessimistic works of many contemporary writers of this mode.*

*In his play entitled "Luv" he satirizes the dishonest way in which many people experience love. This play was extremely well received.*

*Schisgal often uses comedy to get at his serious statements. The humor of "The Pushcart Peddlers" (1980) is an excellent example of his genius in this vein.*

*Among his well-known works are "The Typists" and "The Tiger" (both of which started his career as a dramatist in 1960), "Luv" (1963), "The Old Jew" (1965), "Jimmy Shine" (1969) and "The Chinese" (1970). Several of his plays have been made into films, and he has won various awards. "The Pushcart Peddlers" was published in "The Best Short Plays", 1981.*

**Annotations**

**5** **pushcart peddlers** men who move about selling small quantities of goods from two-wheeled vehicles which they push – 10 **backdrop** *Hintergrund-vorhang* – 13 **keg** small barrel – **crate** box for transporting goods – 16 **ragtime** popular music of black American origin – 18 **baggy** hanging loosely – **soiled derby** dirty bowler (hat) – 22 **battered** in poor condition due to hard usage – **threadbare** [ˈθredbɛə] worn thin; shabby – **wilted** no longer fresh (said usually of plants) – 25 **to peek** to take a short, quick look, often secretly – 30 **expansive** [ɪksˈpænsɪv] not holding back

**6** 1 **rotten** *(sl.)* bad – 3 **to snap s.th. open** to open s.th. (like a bag) with a quick turn of the wrist – 14 **celebrity** [sɪˈlebrɪtɪ] s.o. famous – 18 **the nerve of some people** *(coll.)* some people don't know the limits of proper behavior – 19 **to make a spectacle of o.s.** to draw attention to o.s. by behaving ridiculously – 32 **vicinity** [vɪˈsɪnɪtɪ] *nähere Umgebung* – 35 **mop** s.th. with which to dust, usually made out of cloth or feathers

**7** 1 **to get off the boat** (from Europe); "just off the boat" (figurative expression): completely new to America – 2 **a stroke of good luck** [strəʊk] an unexpected happy event – 15 **cigar butt** [sɪˈgɑːˌbʌt] last remains of a cigar – 16 **marvelous** [ˈmɑːvələs] astonishing; wonderful – 19 **Catskill Mountains** low range of mountains northwest of New York City; favorite vacationing area of New York Jews early in this century – 27 **I would appreciate that** [əˈpriːʃɪeɪt] I would like that very much

**8** 10 **brand new** absolutely new – **legitimate** lawful; reasonable – **to prosper** to be successful – 17 **initial** (= initial letter) [ɪˈnɪʃl] first letter of a word, a name – 28 **it goes to show** it proves – 29 **indignant** [ɪnˈdɪgnənt] angry and scornful – 35 **to chat** to talk with s.o. about unimportant things

**9** 3 **decent** [ˈdiːsnt] respectable; *(coll.)* satisfactory, good – 5 **tinsmith** *Klempner* – **carpenter** person who works with wood – 7 **blockhead** [ˈblɒkhed] *(sl.)* slow and stupid person – 16 **to grab** to take quickly – 19 **to use the old noodle** *(sl.)* (referring to the brain:) to be inventive, clever – 26 **to make a go of s.th.** *(coll.)* to be successful at s.th. – 36 **distinctive** [–ˈ––] special – 38 **to jerk** to move suddenly, quickly

**10** 2 **to tip** (a hat:) to lift a hat slightly off the head in a gesture of politeness – 12 **to make a fortune** to become rich

**11** 6 **to give s.o. a fair shake** *(sl.)* to give s.o. a good financial deal – 10 **proprietary** [–ˈ–––] like an owner – 14 **avalanche** [ˈ–––] *Lawine* – 15 **undismayed** undiscouraged – 18 **to gape** to stare open-mouthed and in surprise – 19 **replica** [ˈ–––] copy – 27 **to hurl** to throw with great energy – 28 **groom** man who is getting married – **brawl ensues** [brɔːl] fight follows – **to**

**hawk** to hawk a laugh: *here* to laugh from the throat – 31 **merchandise** goods to be sold – 35 **bankruptcy proceedings** ['bæŋkrəptsɪ prə'si:dɪŋz] legal procedure for going out of business – 40 **(to be) considerate** [kən'sɪdərət] to respect s.o. else's needs and desires

**12**  4 **location** [lə'keɪʃn] place

**13**  3 **to negotiate** to talk things over in a formal way – 11 **to whittle** ['wɪtl] to reduce by degrees – 12 **nil** nothing – **equitable** ['ekwɪtəbl] fair, just – 16 **in contradistinction to** (extremely formal) as opposed to

**14**  4 **to coach s.o.** to help s.o. – 5 **to be hard up** *(coll.)* in a bad situation for financial reasons – 9 **broke** *(sl.)* out of money – 11 **to pace** to walk with slow, regular steps (usually back and forth) – 12 **on the verge of** very close to – 13 **the old country** that part of Europe from which o.s. or one's ancestors came – 14 **elderly** ['eldəlɪ] rather old – **to be confined to (one's bed)** to be unable to leave (one's bed) – 15 **bursitis** [bə'saɪtɪs] *Schleimbeutelentzündung* – 17 **sob** [sɒb] *Schluchzen* – 20 **to weep** to cry – 21 **affliction** cause or occasion of suffering – 30 **to embrace** to take (a person) into one's arms – 38 **horsing around** *(sl.)* foolish play, often somewhat wild

**15**  17 **to get a swollen head** to become too proud of o.s. – 22 **frock** dress or gown – 23 **strapped around** attached to – 25 **angelic** [–'– –] like an angel – 27 **perspiring** [pə'spaɪərɪŋ] sweating – 38 **destitute** ['destɪtju:t] extremely poor

**16**  7 **fucking** (vulgar) term often used as a swear word to add emphasis to what is said – 9 **to retrieve** [rɪ'tri:v] to get back – 11 **to poke out** [pəʊk] to make a hole by pushing s.th. in or through – 14 **Buster!** ['bʌstə] *(sl.)* mister, fellow (has a somewhat rough, insulting connotation) – **whore** (contemptuous term for a) prostitute – 17 **how the hell** *(sl.)* how in the world – **gonna** *(substandard)* going to – 20 **lousy** *(sl.)* disgusting, bad – 23 **orphan** child who has lost one or both of its parents by death – 24 **you bet …** *(sl.)* sure, certainly – 26 **stinkweed** (weed = *Unkraut*) strong-scented or ill-smelling plant – 28 **self-conscious** [ˌself'kɒnʃəs] insecure, shy – 30 **that figures** *(coll.)* that makes sense – **crumb-bum** a worthless person – **creep** *(sl.)* a disagreeable person – 31 **to bop** *(sl.)* to hit – 33 **I hate your (lousy) guts!** (extremely strong expression of dislike for s.o.) – guts = intestines *(Eingeweide)* – 36 **to apologize** [ə'pɒlədʒaɪz] to say you are sorry – **ma'am** = madam – 37 **he has no sense of propriety** [prə'praɪətɪ] he doesn't know how to behave – 39 **decency** ['di:snsɪ] respectable behaviour in society – 40 **to dump** to throw (away) carelessly

**17**  6 **dejectedly** [dɪ'dʒektɪdlɪ] sadly – 7 **to bow** [baʊ] (done by males) to bend over in a gesture of polite formality – 9 **to curtsy** ['kɜtsɪ] (done by females) to make a movement of respect (by bending the knees) – **pleased to make your**

**acquaintance** [ə'kweɪntəns] (quite formal) glad to meet you – 11 **to sustain o.s.** [səs'teɪn] to earn money to live – 12 **thespian** ['θespɪən] actor/actress – **tap dancer** *Steptänzer* – **highly regarded chanteuse** highly respected singer – **transitional** [træn'sɪʒənl] changing from one state into another – 15 **genuine ambition** ['dʒenjʊɪn] true desire/goal – **Stock Exchange** *Börse* – 31 **to purchase** to buy – 37 **premature** [ˌpremə'tjʊə] *here:* too early – 38 **foreseeable future** near future

**8** 3 **to be frank with you** quite honestly – 7 **without reservation** without holding back, without doubts – 9 **obligations** responsibilities – 12 **beer-belly** big, fat stomach – 25 **iodine** ['aɪədɪn, *A.E.* 'aɪədaɪn] *Jod* – 28 **to bear** to endure; tolerate – 32 **savior** ['seɪvɪə] (*B.E.* saviour) person who delivers s.o. from harm or danger – 33 **that's a riot** *(sl.)* that's extremely funny

**9** 2 **repressed person** person who suffers from psychological blockages – 8 **shenanigan** *(coll.)* foolery – **willy-nilly** without choice – 9 **brat** (contemptuous) misbehaved child – 10 **gypsy** ['dʒɪpsɪ] *Zigeuner(in)* – 18 **to be the laughing stock** to be laughed at by everyone – 25 **cancer** *Krebs* – 27 **an I.O.U.** (short for:) I owe you = piece of paper in which one acknowledges debt – **lien** [lɪən] a legal claim upon property until the owner has repaid a loan or debt – 31 **to plead** to ask earnestly

**0** 4 **Shirley Temple** famous American child actress in the 1930's – 5 **to pant** to take short, quick breaths – 12 **posture** ['pɒstʃə] way the body is held – 13 **pronounced** strongly marked, distinct – **sophistication** [səˌfɪstɪ'keɪʃn] refined behavior – 15 **to dilly-dally** ['dɪlɪ'dælɪ] to play around – 16 **curt** [kɜːt] brief, often to the point of rudeness – 19 **clenched** closed tightly – 22 **to da-da** to replace the words of a song with "da" – **to whirl** [wɜːl] to spin – 23 **to stumble** to fall almost – **noteworthy** ['nəʊtwɜːðɪ] significant – 24 **verdict** ['vɜːdɪkt] judgment, decision – 28 **fervent** ['fɜːvənt] very passionate

**1** 2 **relentless** [rɪ'lentlɪs] without pity – 16 **bite** *Bissen, Happen* – 20 **incredible** [ɪn'kredɪbl] unbelievable – 22 **head-over-heels** *(coll.)* completely – 17 **casserole** ['kæsərəʊl] food, usually a mixture, cooked in a covered dish of glass or pottery (Auflauf) – 24 **to have one's heart in one's mouth** to be greatly excited or frightened – 25 **over a hundred** (degrees Fahrenheit; about 38.5 centigrade) – 27 **to pinch** *zwicken* – 37 **dedication** [ˌdedɪ'keɪʃn] strong interest in and devotion to s.th.

**2** 1 **incredulous** [ɪn'kredjʊləs] unbelieving – 7 **conservative** *here:* cautiously moderate, not enterprising enough – 12 **simultaneous** [ˌsɪməl'teɪnɪəs, *A.E.* ˌsaɪməl'teɪnɪəs] – 13 **to punctuate** ['pʌŋktjʊeɪt] *here:* to interrupt from time to time

Thornton Wilder

# The Happy Journey
# to Trenton and Camden

Characters

THE STAGE MANAGER
MA KIRBY
ARTHUR *(thirteen)*
5      CAROLINE *(fifteen)*
PA (ELMER) KIRBY
BEULAH *(twenty-two)*

*No scenery is required for this play. The idea is that no place is being*
*represented. This may be achieved by a gray curtain back-drop with no*
10    *side-pieces; a cyclorama; or the empty bare stage.*

*(As the curtain rises the stage manager is leaning lazily against the pro-*
*scenium pillar at the left. He is smoking. Arthur is playing marbles down*
*center in pantomime. Caroline is way up left talking to some girls who are*
*invisible to us. Ma Kirby is anxiously putting on her hat [real] before an*
15    *imaginary mirror up right.)*

MA    Where's your pa? Why isn't he here? I declare we'll never get started.
ARTHUR    Ma, where's my hat? I guess I don't go if I can't find my hat.

*(Still playing marbles.)*

MA    Go out into the hall and see if it isn't there. Where's Caroline gone to
20    now, the plagued child?
ARTHUR    She's out waitin' in the street talkin' to the Jones girls. – I just
looked in the hall a thousand times, Ma, and it isn't there. *(He spits for*
*good luck before a difficult shot and mutters.)*    Come on, baby.
MA    Go and look again, I say. Look carefully.

25    *(Arthur rises, reluctantly, crosses right, turns around, returns swiftly to his*
*game center, flinging himself on the floor with a terrible impact, and starts*
*shooting an aggie.)*

ARTHUR    No, Ma, it's not there.

MA *(serenely):* Well, you don't leave Newark without that hat, make up your mind to that. I don't go on journeys with a hoodlum.

ARTHUR Aw, Ma!

*(Ma comes down right to the footlights, pulls up an imaginary window and*
5 *talks toward the audience.)*

MA *(calling):* Oh, Mrs. Schwartz!

THE STAGE MANAGER *(down left. Consulting his script):* Here I am, Mrs. Kirby. Are you going yet?

MA I guess we're going in just a minute. How's the baby?

10 THE STAGE MANAGER She's all right now. We slapped her on the back and she spat it up.

MA Isn't that fine! – Well, now, if you'll be good enough to give the cat a saucer of milk in the morning and the evening, Mrs. Schwartz, I'll be ever so grateful to you. – Oh, good-afternoon, Mrs. Hobmeyer!

15 THE STAGE MANAGER Good-afternoon, Mrs. Kirby, I hear you're going away.

MA *(modest):* Oh, just for three days, Mrs. Hobmeyer, to see my married daughter, Beulah, in Camden. Elmer's got his vacation week from the laundry early this year, and he's just the best driver in the world.

20 *(Caroline comes down stage right and stands by her mother.)*

THE STAGE MANAGER Is the whole family going?

MA Yes, all four of us that's here. The change ought to be good for the children. My married daughter was downright sick a while ago –

THE STAGE MANAGER Tchk – tchk – tchk! Yes. I remember you tellin' us.

25 MA *(with feeling):* And I just want to go down and see the child. I ain't seen her since then. I just won't rest easy in my mind without I see her. (To Caroline) Can't you say good-afternoon to Mrs. Hobmeyer?

CAROLINE *(lowers her eyes and says woodenly):* Good-afternoon, Mrs. Hobmeyer.

30 THE STAGE MANAGER Good-afternoon, dear. – Well, I'll wait and beat these rugs until after you're gone, because I don't want to choke you. I hope you have a good time and find everything all right.

MA Thank you, Mrs. Hobmeyer, I hope I will. – Well, I guess that milk for the cat is all, Mrs. Schwartz, if you're sure you don't mind. If anything
35 should come up, the key to the back door is hanging by the ice-box.

CAROLINE Ma! Not so loud.

ARTHUR Everybody can hear yuh.

MA Stop pullin' my dress, children. *(In a loud whisper.)* The key to the

back door I'll leave hangin' by the ice-box and I'll leave the screen un-
hooked.

THE STAGE MANAGER   Now have a good trip, dear, and give my love to
Beuhly.

5   MA   I will, and thank you a thousand times. *(She lowers the window, turns
up stage, and looks around. Caroline goes left and vigorously rubs her
cheeks. Ma occupies herself with the last touches of packing.)*   What can
be keeping your pa?

ARTHUR *(who has not left his marbles):*   I can't find my hat, Ma.

10   *(Enter Elmer holding a cap, up right.)*

ELMER   Here's Arthur's hat. He musta left it in the car Sunday.

MA   That's a mercy. Now we can start. – Caroline Kirby, what you done to
your cheeks?

CAROLINE *(defiant-abashed):*   Nothin'.

15   MA   If you've put anything on 'em, I'll slap you.

CAROLINE   No, Ma, of course I haven't. *(Hanging her head.)*   I just rub-
bed 'm to make 'm red. All the girls do that at High School when they're
goin' places.

MA   Such silliness I never saw. Elmer, what kep' you?

20   ELMER *(always even-voiced and always looking out a little anxiously through
his spectacles):*   I just went to the garage and had Charlie give a last look
at it, Kate.

MA   I'm glad you did. *Collecting two pieces of imaginary luggage and
starting for the door.)*   I wouldn't like to have no breakdown miles from

25   anywhere. Now we can start. Arthur, put those marbles away. Anybody'd think you didn't want to go on a journey to look at yuh.

*(They go out through the "hall". Ma opens imaginary door down right.
Pa, Caroline, and Arthur go through it. Ma follows, taking time to lock the
door, hang the key by the "ice-box." They turn up at an abrupt angle,*

30   *going up stage. As they come to the steps from the back porch, each
arriving at a given point, starts bending his knees lower and lower to denote
going downstairs, and find themselves in the street. The stage manager
moves from the right to the automobile. It is right center of the stage, seen
partially at an angle, its front pointing down center.*

35   ELMER *(coming forward):*   Here, you boys, you keep away from that car.

MA   Those Sullivan boys put their heads into everything.

*(They get into the car. Elmer's hands hold an imaginary steering wheel and continually shift gears. Ma sits beside him. Arthur is behind him and Caroline is behind Ma.)*

5  CAROLINE *(standing up in the back seat, waving self-consciously):*  Good-bye, Mildred. Good-bye, Helen.

THE STAGE MANAGER *(having returned to his position by the left proscenium):*  Good-bye, Caroline. Good-bye, Mrs. Kirby. I hope y' have a good time.

MA  Good-bye, girls.

THE STAGE MANAGER  Good-bye, Kate. The car looks fine.

10  MA *(looking upward toward a window right):*  Oh, good-bye, Emma! *(Modestly.)*  We think it's the best little Chevrolet in the world. – *(Looking up toward the left.)*  Oh, good-bye, Mrs. Adler!

THE STAGE MANAGER  What, are you going away, Mrs. Kirby?

15  MA  Just for three days, Mrs. Adler, to see my married daughter in Camden.

THE STAGE MANAGER  Have a good time.

*(Now Ma, Caroline, and the Stage Manager break out into a tremendous chorus of good-byes. The whole street is saying good-bye. Arthur takes out*
20  *his pea shooter and lets fly happily into the air. There is a lurch or two and they are off.)*

ARTHUR *(leaning forward in sudden fright):*  Pa! Pa! Don't go by the school. Mr. Biedenbach might see us!

MA  I don't care if he does see us. I guess I can take my children out of
25  school for one day without having to hide down back streets about it. *(Elmer nods to a passerby. Without sharpness.)*  Who was that you spoke to, Elmer?

ELMER  That was the fellow who arranges our banquets down to the Lodge, Kate.

30  MA  Is he the one who had to buy four hundred steaks? *(Pa nods.)*  I declare, I'm glad I'm not him.

ELMER  The air's getting better already. Take deep breaths, children.

*(They inhale noisily.)*

ARTHUR *(pointing to a sign and indicating that it gradually goes by):*  Gee,
35  it's almost open fields already. *"Weber and Heilbroner Suits for Well-dressed Men."*  Ma, can I have one of them some day?

MA   If you graduate with good marks perhaps your father'll let you have
one for graduation.

*(Pause. General gazing about, then sudden lurch.)*

CAROLINE *(whining):*   Oh, Pa! do we have to wait while that whole funeral
5   goes by?

*(Elmer takes off his hat. Ma cranes forward with absorbed curiosity.)*

MA *(not sharp and bossy):*   Take off your hat, Arthur. Look at your father.
– Why, Elmer, I do believe that's a lodge-brother of yours. See the
banner? I suppose this is the Elizabeth branch. *(Elmer nods. Ma sighs:*
10   *Tchk-tchk-tchk. The children lean forward and all watch the funeral in
silence, growing momentarily more solemnized. After a pause, Ma continues almost dreamily but not sentimentally.)*   Well, we haven't forgotten
the funeral that we went on, have we? We haven't forgotten our good
Harold. He gave his life for this country, we mustn't forget that. *(There
15   is another pause; with cheerful resignation.)*   Well, we'll all hold up the
traffic for a few minutes some day.

THE CHILDREN *(very uncomfortable):*   Ma!

MA *(without self-pity):*   Well, I'm "ready," children. I hope everybody in
this car is "ready." And I pray to go first, Elmer. Yes.

20   *(Elmer touches her hand.)*

CAROLINE   Ma, everybody's looking at you.

ARTHUR   Everybody's laughing at you.

MA   Oh, hold your tongues! I don't care what a lot of silly people in
Elizabeth, New Jersey, think of me. – Now we can go on. That's the last.

25   *(There is another lurch and the car goes on.)*

CAROLINE *(looking at a sign and turning as she passes it):* "Fit-Rite Suspenders. The Working Man's Choice."   Pa, why do they spell Rite that way?

ELMER   So that it'll make you stop and ask about it, Missy.

CAROLINE   Papa, you're teasing me. – Ma, why do they say *"Three
30   Hundred Rooms Three Hundred Baths"?*

ARTHUR *"Miller's Spaghetti: The Family's Favorite Dish."*   Ma, why don't
you ever have spaghetti?

MA   Go along, you'd never eat it.

ARTHUR   Ma, I like it now.

35   CAROLINE *(with gesture):*   Yum-yum. It looked wonderful up there. Ma,
make some when we get home?

MA *(dryly):* "The management is always happy to receive suggestions. We aim to please."

*(The children scream with laughter. Even Elmer smiles. Ma remains modest.)*

5 ELMER  Well, I guess no one's complaining, Kate. Everybody knows you're a good cook.

MA  I don't know whether I'm a good cook or not, but I know I've had practice. At least I've cooked three meals a day for twenty-five years.

ARTHUR  Aw, Ma, you went out to eat once in a while.

10 MA  Yes. That made it a leap year.

*(The children laugh again.)*

CAROLINE *(in an ecstasy of well-being puts her arms around her mother):*  Ma, I love going out in the country like this. Let's do it often, Ma.

15 MA  Goodness, smell that air, will you! It's got the whole ocean in it. – Elmer, drive careful over that bridge. This must be New Brunswick we're coming to.

ARTHUR *(after a slight pause):*  Ma, when is the next comfort station?

MA *(unruffled):*  You don't want one. You just said that to be awful.

20 CAROLINE *(shrilly):*  Yes, he did, Ma. He's terrible. He says that kind of thing right out in school and I want to sink through the floor, Ma. He's terrible.

MA  Oh, don't get so excited about nothing, Miss Proper! I guess we're all yewman beings in this car, at least as far as I know. And, Arthur, you try
25 and be a gentleman. – Elmer, don't run over that collie dog. *She follows the dog with her eyes.)*  Looked kinda peaked to me. Needs a good honest bowl of leavings. Pretty dog, too. *(Her eyes fall on a billboard at the right.)*  That's a pretty advertisement for Chesterfield cigarettes, isn't it? Looks like Beulah, a little.

30 ARTHUR  Ma?

MA  Yes.

ARTHUR *("route" rhymes with "out"):*  Can't I take a paper route with the Newark *Daily Post?*

MA  No, you cannot. No, sir. I hear they make the paper boys get up four-
35 thirty in the morning. No son of mine is going to get up at four-thirty every morning, not if it's to make a million dollars. Your *Saturday Evening Post* route on Thursday mornings is enough.

ARTHUR  Aw, Ma.

MA   No, sir. No son of mine is going to get up at four-thirty and miss the sleep God meant him to have.

ARTHUR *(sullenly):*   Hhm! Ma's always talking about God. I guess she got a letter from Him this morning.

5   MA *(outraged):*   Elmer, stop that automobile this minute. I don't go another step with anybody that says things like that. Arthur, you get out of this car. *(Elmer stops the car.)*  Elmer, you give him a dollar bill. He can go back to Newark by himself. I don't want him.

ARTHUR   What did I say? There wasn't anything terrible about that.

10   ELMER   I didn't hear what he said, Kate.

MA   God has done a lot of things for me and I won't have Him made fun of by anybody. Get out of this car this minute.

CAROLINE   Aw, Ma – don't spoil the ride.

MA   No.

15   ELMER   We might as well go on, Kate, since we've got started. I'll talk to the boy tonight.

MA *(slowly conceding):*   All right, if you say so, Elmer.

*(Elmer starts the car.)*

ARTHUR *(frightened):*   Aw, Ma, that wasn't so terrible.

20   MA   I don't want to talk about it. I hope your father washes your mouth out with soap and water. – Where'd we all be if I started talking about God like that, I'd like to know! We'd be in the speakeasies and nightclubs and places like that, that's where we'd be.

CAROLINE *(after a very slight pause):*   What did he say, Ma? I didn't hear
25   what he said.

MA   I don't want to talk about it.

*(They drive on in silence for a moment, the shocked silence after a scandal.)*

ELMER   I'm going to stop and give the car a little water, I guess.

30   MA   All right, Elmer. You know best.

ELMER *(turns the wheel and stops; as to a garage hand)*   Could I have a little water in the radiator – to make sure?

THE STAGE MANAGER *(in this scene alone he lays aside his script and enters into a rôle seriously)*   You sure can. *(He punches the left front tire.)*  Air
35   all right? Do you need any oil or gas?

*(Goes up around car.)*

ELMER   No, I think not. I just got fixed up in Newark.

*(The Stage Manager carefully pours some water into the hood.)*

MA   We're on the right road for Camden, are we?

THE STAGE MANAGER *(coming down on right side of car)*   Yes, keep straight
ahead. You can't miss it. You'll be in Trenton in a few minutes. Cam-
5   den's a great town, lady, believe me.

MA   My daughter likes it fine – my married daughter.

THE STAGE MANAGER   Ye'? It's a great burg all right. I guess I think so
because I was born near there.

MA   Well, well. Your folks still live there?

10   THE STAGE MANAGER *(standing with one foot on the rung of Ma's chair. They
have taken a great fancy to one another)*   No, my old man sold the farm
and they built a factory on it. So the folks moved to Philadelphia.

MA   My married daughter Beulah lives there because her husband works in
the telephone company. – Stop pokin' me, Caroline! – We're all going
15   down to see her for a few days.

THE STAGE MANAGER   Ye'?

MA   She's been sick, you see, and I just felt I had to go and see her. My
husband and my boy are going to stay at the Y.M.C.A. I hear they've got
a dormitory on the top floor that's real clean and comfortable. Have you
20   ever been there?

THE STAGE MANAGER   No. I'm Knights of Columbus myself.

MA   Oh.

THE STAGE MANAGER   I used to play basketball at the Y though. It looked
all right to me. *(He reluctantly moves away and pretends to examine the
25   car again.)*   Well, I guess you're all set now, lady. I hope you have a good
trip; you can't miss it.

EVERYBODY   Thanks. Thanks a lot. Good luck to you.

*(Jolts and lurches.)*

MA *(with a sigh)*   The world's full of nice people. – That's what I call a nice
30   young man.

CAROLINE *(earnestly)*   Ma, you oughtn't to tell 'm all everything about
yourself.

MA   Well, Caroline, you do your way and I'll do mine. – He looked kinda
pale to me. I'd like to feed him up for a few days. His mother lives in
35   Philadelphia and I expect he eats at those dreadful Greek places.

CAROLINE   I'm hungry. Pa, there's a hot dog stand. K'n I have one?

ELMER   We'll all have one, eh, Kate? We had such an early lunch.

MA   Just as you think best, Elmer.

*(Elmer stops the car.)*

ELMER   Arthur, here's half a dollar. – Run over and see what they have. Not too much mustard either.

5   *(Arthur descends from the car and goes off stage right. Ma and Caroline get out and walk a bit, up stage and to the left. Caroline keeps at her mother's right.)*

MA   What's that flower over there? – I'll take some of those to Beulah.
CAROLINE   It's just a weed, Ma.

MA   I like it. – My, look at the sky, wouldya! I'm glad I was born in New
10   Jersey. I've always said it was the best state in the Union. Every state has something no other state has got.

*(Presently Arthur returns with his hands full of imaginary hot dogs which he distributes. First to his father, next to Caroline, who comes forward to meet him, and lastly to his mother. He is still very much cast down by the*
15   *recent scandal, and as he approaches his mother says falteringly):*
ARTHUR   Ma, I'm sorry. I'm sorry. I'm sorry for what I said.

*(He bursts into tears.)*

MA   There. There. We all say wicked things at times. I know you didn't mean it like it sounded. *(He weeps still more violently than before.)*
20   Why, now, now! I forgive you, Arthur, and tonight before you go to bed you ... *(She whispers.)*   You're a good boy at heart, Arthur, and we all know it. *(Caroline starts to cry too. Ma is suddenly joyously alive and happy.)*   Sakes alive, it's too nice a day for us all to be cryin'. Come now, get in. *(Crossing behind car to the right side, followed by the children.)*
25   Caroline, go up in front with your father. Ma wants to sit with her beau. *(Caroline sits in front with her father. Ma lets Arthur get in car ahead of her; then she closes door.)*   I never saw such children. Your hot dogs are all getting wet. Now chew them fine, everybody. – All right, Elmer, forward march. *(Car starts. Caroline spits.)*   Caroline, whatever are you
30   doing?
CAROLINE   I'm spitting out the leather, Ma.
MA   Then say: Excuse me.
CAROLINE   Excuse me, please.

*(She spits again.)*

35   MA   What's this place? Arthur, did you see the post office?
ARTHUR   It said Lawrenceville.

MA   Hhn. School kinda. Nice. I wonder what that big yellow house set back
was. – Now it's beginning to be Trenton.

CAROLINE   Papa, it was near here that George Washington crossed the
Delaware. It was near Trenton, Mama. He was first in war and first in
5   peace, and first in the hearts of his countrymen.

MA   *(surveying the passing world, serene and didactic)*   Well the thing I like
about him best was that he never told a lie.   *(The children are duly cast
down. There is a pause. Arthur stands up and looks at the car ahead.)*
There's a sunset for you. There's nothing like a good sunset.

10   ARTHUR   There's an Ohio license in front of us. Ma, have you ever been to
Ohio?

MA   No.

*(A dreamy silence descends upon them. Caroline sits closer to her father,
toward the left; Arthur closer to Ma on the right, who puts her arm around
15   him, unsentimentally.)*

ARTHUR   Ma, what a lotta people there are in the world, Ma. There must
be thousands and thousands in the United States. Ma, how many are
there?

MA   I don't know. Ask your father.

20   ARTHUR   Pa, how many are there?

ELMER   There are a hundred and twenty-six million, Kate.

MA   *(giving a pressure about Arthur's shoulder)*   And they all like to drive
out in the evening with their children beside 'm. Why doesn't somebody
sing something? Arthur, you're always singing something; what's the
25   matter with you?

ARTHUR   All right. What'll we sing?

*(He sketches.)*

In the Blue Ridge Mountains of Virginia,
On the ...

30   No, I don't like that anymore. Let's do:

I been workin' on de railroad
   *(Caroline joins in.)*
All de liblong day.
   *(Ma sings.)*
35   I been workin' on de railroad
   *(Elmer joins in.)*

Just to pass de time away.
Don't you hear de whistle blowin', etc.

*(Ma suddenly jumps up with a wild cry and a large circular gesture.)*

MA   Elmer, that signpost said Camden. I saw it.
5   ELMER   All right, Kate, if you're sure.

*(Much shifting of gears, backing, and jolting.)*

MA   Yes, there it is. Camden – five miles. Dear old Beulah. *(The journey continues.)* Now, children, you be good and quiet during dinner. She's just got out of bed after a big sorta operation, and we must all move
10   around kinda quiet. First you drop me and Caroline at the door and just say hello, and the you men-folk go over to the Y.M.C.A. and come back for dinner in about an hour.
CAROLINE *(shutting her eyes and pressing her fists passionately against her nose)*   I see the first star. Everybody make a wish.

15   Star light, star bright,
First star I seen tonight.
I wish I may, I wish I might
Have the wish I wish tonight.

*(Then solemnly.)*   Pins. Mama, you say "needles."

20   *(She interlocks little fingers with her mother across back of seat.)*

MA   Needles.
CAROLINE   Shakespeare. Ma, you say "Longfellow."
MA   Longfellow.
CAROLINE   Now it's a secret and I can't tell it to anybody. Ma, you make a
25   wish.
MA *(with almost grim humor)*   No, I can make wishes without waiting for no star. And I can tell my wishes right out loud too. Do you want to hear them?
CAROLINE *(resignedly)*   No, Ma, we know 'm already. We've heard 'm.
30   *(She hangs her head affectedly on her left shoulder and says with unmali-cious mimicry.)*   You want me to be a good girl and you want Arthur to be honest-in-word-and-deed.
MA *(majestically)*   Yes. So mind yourself.
ELMER   Caroline, take out that letter from Beulah in my coat pocket by you
35   and read aloud the places I marked with red pencil.

CAROLINE *(laboriously making it out)* *"A few blocks after you pass the two big oil tanks on your left ..."*

EVERYBODY *(pointing backward)* There they are!

CAROLINE *"... you come to a corner where there's an A and P store on the
5  left and a firehouse kitty-corner to it ..."* *(They all jubilantly identify these landmarks.)* *"... turn right, go two blocks and our house is Weyerhauser St. Number 471."*

MA   It's an even nicer street than they used to live in. And right handy to an A and P.

10 CAROLINE *(whispering)* Ma, it's better than our street. It's richer than our street. Ma, isn't Beulah richer than we are?

MA *(looking at her with a firm and glassy eye)* Mind yourself, Missy. I don't want to hear anybody talking about rich or not rich when I'm around. If people aren't nice I don't care how rich they are. I live in the best street in
15  the world because my husband and children live there. *(She glares impressively at Caroline a moment to let this lesson sink in, then looks up, sees Beulah off left, and waves.)* There's Beulah standing on the steps looking for us.

*(Beulah enters from left, also waving. They all call out: "Hello, Beulah –*
20  *hello." Presently they are all getting out of the car, except Elmer, busy with brakes.)*

BEULAH   Hello, Mamma. Well, lookit how Arthur and Caroline are growing.

MA   They're bursting all their clothes.

25 BEULAH *(crossing in front of them and kissing her father long and affectionately)* Hello, Papa. Good old papa. You look tired, Pa.

MA   Yes, your pa needs a rest. Thank Heaven, his vacation has come just now. We'll feed him up and let him sleep late. *(Elmer gets out of car and stands in front of it.)* Pa has a present for you, Loolie. He would go and
30  buy it.

BEULAH   Why, Pa, you're terrible to go and buy anything for me. Isn't he terrible?

*(Stage Manager removes automobile.)*

MA   Well, it's a secret. You can open it at dinner.

35 BEULAH *(puts her arm around his neck and rubs her nose against his temple)* Crazy old pa, goin' buyin' things! It's me that oughta be buyin' things for you, Pa.

ELMER   Oh, no! There's only one Loolie in the world.

BEULAH *(whispering, as her eyes fill with tears)*  Are you glad I'm still alive, Pa?

*(She kisses him abruptly and goes back to the house steps.)*

ELMER  Where's Horace, Loolie?

5  BEULAH  He was kep' a little at the office. He'll be here any minute. He's crazy to see you all.

MA  All right. You men go over to the Y and come back in about an hour.

BEULAH  Go straight along, Pa, you can't miss it. It just stares at yuh. *(Elmer and Arthur exit down right.)*  Well, come on upstairs, Ma, and
10  take your things. – Caroline, there's a surprise for you in the back yard.

CAROLINE  Rabbits?

BEULAH  No.

CAROLINE  Chickins?

BEULAH  No. Go and see. *(Caroline runs off stage, down left.)*  There are
15  two new puppies. You be thinking over whether you can keep one in Newark.

MA  I guess we can. *(Ma and Beulah turn and walk way up stage right. The Stage Manager pushes out a cot from the left, and places it down left on a slant so that its foot is toward the left. Beulah and Ma come down stage
20  center toward left.)*  It's a nice house, Beulah. You just got a lovely home.

BEULAH  When I got back from the hospital, Horace had moved everything into it, and there wasn't anything for me to do.

MA  It's lovely.

25  *(Beulah sits on the cot, testing the springs.)*

BEULAH  I think you'll find this comfortable, Ma. *(Beulah sits on down stage end of it.)*

MA *(taking off her hat)*  Oh, I could sleep on a heapa shoes, Loolie! I don't have no trouble sleepin'. *(She sits down up stage of her.)*  Now let me
30  look at my girl. Well, well, when I last saw you, you didn't know me. You kep' saying: *When's Mama comin'? When's Mama comin'?* But the doctor sent me away.

BEULAH *(puts her head on her mother's shoulder and weeps)*  It was awful, Mama. It was awful. She didn't even live a few minutes, Mama. It was
35  awful.

MA *(in a quick, light, urgent undertone)*  God thought best, dear. God thought best. We don't understand why. We just go on, honey, doin' our business. *(Then almost abruptly.)* Well, now *(stands up)*, what are we giving the men to eat tonight?

BEULAH There's a chicken in the oven.

MA What time didya put it in?

5 BEULAH *(restraining her)* Aw, Ma, don't go yet. *(Taking her mother's hand and drawing her down beside her.)* I like to sit here with you this way. You always get the fidgets when we try and pet yuh, Mama.

MA *(ruefully, laughing)* Yes, it's kinda foolish. I'm just an old Newark bag-a-bones.

0 *(She glances at the backs of her hands.)*

BEULAH *(indignantly)* Why, Ma, you're good-lookin'! We always said you were good-lookin'. – And besides, you're the best ma we could ever have.

MA *(uncomfortable)* Well, I hope you like me. There's nothin' like bein'

5 liked by your family. – *(Rises.)* Now I'm going downstairs to look at the chicken. You stretch out here for a minute and shut your eyes. *(She helps Beulah to a lying position.)* Have you got everything laid in for breakfast before the shops close?

BEULAH Oh, you know! Ham and eggs.

0 *(They both laugh. Ma puts an imaginary blanket over Beulah.)*

MA I declare I never could understand what men see in ham and eggs. I think they're horrible. – What time did you put the chicken in?

BEULAH Five o'clock.

MA Well, now, you shut your eyes for ten minutes.

5 *(Ma turns, walks directly up stage, then along the back wall to the right as she absent-mindedly and indistinctly sings):*

There were ninety and nine that safely lay
In the shelter of the fold ...

*and the curtain falls*

## Biographical Notes

*Thornton Wilder was born in 1897 to parents who were both seriously religious: his father was a Congregationalist who insisted on Puritan virtues and his mother was the daughter of a Presbyterian minister. He was strongly influenced by their beliefs.*

*Wilder attended Oberlin College and then transferred to Yale. He contributed substantially to the literary magazine of each college, having by then found his true vocation. While on an archaeological dig in Italy, he participated in the unearthing of an Etruscan street, which deeply influenced him by making clear to him the larger context in which to view the human condition.*

*The attempt to view man's existence in a larger historical and philosophical framework found expression in his literary works, among them "Our Town" (1938), which won Wilder one of the three Pulitzer Prizes he was awarded in his lifetime. The radically bare stage of "Our Town", also found in "The Happy Journey", allows for a symbolism which makes the stage represent the world. In 1928 he won the Pulitzer Prize for his novel "The Bridge of San Luis Rey". Wilder's "The Skin of Our Teeth" won him his third Pulitzer in 1943. It is an imaginative and timeless recapitulation of the entire history of the human race, stressing man's ability to survive somehow, despite the destructive forces of Nature and man's own folly. "The Happy Journey to Trenton and Camden", which Wilder once singled out as his best play, comes from a collection of six one-acters entitled "The Long Christmas Dinner and Other Plays" (1931).*

*Even when working with the provincial, Wilder manages to reach beyond to the universal. He once wrote: "The human adventure is much the same in all times and all places."*

*Thornton Wilder died in 1975.*

## Annotations

**26** 8 **scenery** stage decoration – 9 **back-drop** background – 10 **cyclorama** [ˌsaɪk-ləˈræmə] a large pictorial representation encircling the spectator suggesting unlimited space – 11 **proscenium pillar** [prəʊˈsiːnjəm] a column providing support for the stage structure – 12 **marbles** *Murmeln* – 16 **I declare** *(coll.)* exclamation showing strongly held opinion – 20 **plagued** [pleɪgd] *(dial.)* troublesome – 23 **to mutter** to speak in a low and badly articulated manner – **reluctantly** [–ˈ– – –] in a hesistant way, slowly – 25 **swiftly** quickly – 26 **to fling** to throw with force – **impact** forceful contact – 27 **aggie** [ˈægɪ] a marble

**7** 1 **serenely** [sɪ'ri:nlɪ] calmly – 2 **hoodlum** ['hu:dləm] a rowdy or misbehaved person – 7 **consulting his script** looking at a typed-out version of the play – 11 **spat it up** coughed it up – 14 **grateful** ['greɪtfʊl] feeling or showing thanks – 18 **Beulah** ['bju:lə] from Hebrew, literally meaning married (said of a woman) – 23 **downright** *(sl.)* very – 25 **I ain't** *(sl.) here:* I haven't – **without I see her** *(dial.)* without seeing her – 37 **yuh** *(sl.)* = you

**8** 6 **vigorously** ['vɪgərəslɪ] energetically – 11 **musta** *(sl.)* = must have – 12 **mercy** blessing – **what you done** *(sl.)* what have you done – 14 **defiant-abashed** [dɪ'faɪənt ə'bæʃt] bold and ashamed – 21 **spectacles** glasses – **garage** *A.E.* [gə'rɑ:ʒ] – 23 **luggage** e.g. suitcases, *B.E.* baggage – 24 **I wouldn't like to have no** *(sl.)* I wouldn't like to have any – 30 **porch** a veranda, often in the back or in the front of houses – 31 **denote** [dɪ'nəʊt] *here:* to make it look like …

**9** 2 **to shift gears** [gɪəz] *Gangschaltung betätigen, schalten* – 18 **tremendous** [trə'mendəs] very large – 20 **lurch** to move suddenly – 26 **nod** *nicken* – 28 **banquet** ['bæŋkwɪt] ceremonial or formal dinner – **Lodge** the meeting place of a fraternal organization

**0** 2 **graduation** *(Schul-)Abschluß* – 3 **gazing** looking – 4 **to whine** to complain like a child or a dog – **funeral** ['fju:nərəl] ceremony when s.o. has died – 6 **to crane forward** to stretch one's neck in order to see better – **absorbed** *here:* complete – 9 **banner** a kind of flag – **Elizabeth** town in New Jersey – 11 **solemn** ['sɒləm] serious – 26 **Rite** non-standard orthographic variant of *right* – **suspenders** [səs'pendəz] *Hosenträger* – 28 **Missy** diminutive form of Miss *(kleines Fräulein)* – 29 **to tease** [ti:z] to make fun of s.o., to annoy s.o. – 33 **go along** *(dial.)* 'don't give me that'

**1** 2 **we aim to please** phrase often used in advertisements *(bei uns ist der Kunde König)* – 10 **leap year** the year in which February has 29 days – 18 **comfort station** euphemistic expression referring to public toilets – 19 **unruffled** [ʌn'rʌfld] not upset – 24 **yewman** = human – 26 **peaked** in bad shape, sickly – 27 **leavings** food remaining after a meal – **billboard** a flat surface, generally along roads and highways, on which advertisements are pasted – 32 **paper route** a particular territory in which newspapers are delivered to subscribers *(Abonnenten)*

**2** 3 **sullenly** *here:* disapprovingly – 5 **outraged** extremely angry – 13 **to spoil** to make unsatisfactory – 17 **to concede** [kən'si:d] to give in – 22 **speakeasy** a place where alcoholic drinks were illegally sold (during the years of Prohibition in the United States, 1919–1933) – 30 **garage hand** a person who works at a car repair shop – 31 **radiator** *Kühler* – 33 **to punch** to hit with the fist – 37 **to get fixed up** *(coll.)* to have s.th. checked

**3** 1 **hood** part of car covering engine – 7 **burg** *(A.E., coll.)* city, town – 10 **rung**

*Verstrebung, Sprosse* – 11 **to take a fancy to s.o.** to come to like s.o. very much – 14 **pokin'** = poking; to push s.o. with one's finger – 18 **Y.M.C.A.** *abbrev. for* Young Men's Christian Association – 19 **dormitory** ['dɔ:mɪtrɪ] a large room in which many people sleep – 21 **Knights of Columbus** a fraternal and benevolent society of Roman Catholic men – 23 **the Y** *short for* the Y.M.C.A. – 28 **to jolt** to make an abrupt movement – 33 **kinda** *(spoken language)* = kind of

**34**　8 **weed** *Unkraut* – 10 **the Union** the United States – 14 **cast down** depressed, troubled – 15 **falteringly** hesitatingly, reluctantly – 18 **wicked** ['wɪkɪd] evil – 19 **to weep** to cry – 23 **sakes alive** *(dial.)* an exclamation expressing surprise and/or impatience – 25 **beau** [bəʊ] *(French)* sweetheart, darling

**35**　6 **to survey** to take an inclusive, overall view of s.th. – **didactic** [daɪ'dæktɪk] in a manner appropriate to a teacher – 7 **duly** properly, appropriately – 10 **license** *(short for* "license plate"); metal plate on which a car's registration number is printed – 16 **a lotta** *(sl.)* = a lot of – 33 **liblong** *(dial.)* livelong, i.e. all day long

**36**　9 **sorta** *(informal)* = sort of, kind of – 22 **Longfellow,** Henry Wadsworth, American poet (1807–82) – 26 **grim** serious, stern – 30 **unmalicious mimicry** imitation which does not mean to harm or hurt

**37**　1 **laboriously** [lə'bɔ:rɪəslɪ] with great effort – 4 **A and P** (usually A & P; short for Atlantic and Pacific); U.S. grocery store chain – 5 **kitty-corner** *(coll.)* catty-cornered, diagonally across – **jubilantly** showing great delight, gladness – 12 **glassy** cold, hard – 15 **to glare** to look at s.o. in a severe way – 25 **affectionately** lovingly – 35 **temple** *Schläfe*

**38**　15 **puppy** small dog – 18 **cot** small portable bed *(Feldbett)* – 19 **slant** angle – 28 **heapa** *(sl.)* = heap of, pile of

**39**　4 **didya** *(sl.)* = did you – 5 **to restrain** to hold back – 7 **to get the fidgets** = to fidget; to become nervously, restlessly ill at ease (to fidget = *herumzappeln*) – 8 **rueful** ['ru:fʊl] pitiable, mournful, sad – **bag-a-bones** = bag of bones; a person who looks like he is suffering from hunger – 10 **to glance at** to look at – 11 **indignant** [–'––] a manner expressive of (angry) disapproval – 26 **indistinctly** not clearly – 28 **fold** enclosure for sheep; *here:* group of people with the same religious belief/faith

Tennessee Williams

# The Last of My Solid Gold Watches

This play is inscribed to Mr. Sidney Greenstreet,
for whom the principal character was hopefully conceived.

Characters

MR. CHARLIE COLTON
5     A NEGRO, *a porter in the hotel*
     HARPER, *a traveling salesman*

Scene

*A hotel room in a Mississippi Delta town. The room has looked the same,
with some deterioration, for thirty or forty years. The walls are mustard-*
10   *colored. There are two windows with dull green blinds, torn slightly, a
ceiling-fan, a white iron bed with a pink counterpane, a washstand with
rose-buds painted on the pitcher and bowl, and on the wall a colored
lithograph of blindfolded Hope with her broken lyre.*
     *The door opens and Mr. Charlie Colton comes in. He is a legendary*
15   *character, seventy-eight years old but still "going strong." He is lavish of
flesh, superbly massive and with a kingly dignity of bearing. Once he
moved with a tidal ease and power. Now he puffs and rumbles; when no
one is looking he clasps his hand to his chest and cocks his head to the
warning heart inside him. His huge expanse of chest and belly is criss-*
20   *crossed by multiple gold chains with various little fobs and trinkets
suspended from them. On the back of his head is a derby and in his mouth
a cigar. This is "Mistuh Charlie" – who sadly but proudly refers to himself
as "the last of the Delta drummers." He is followed into the room by a
Negro porter, as old as he is – thin and toothless and grizzled. He totes the*
25   *long orange leather sample cases containing the shoes which Mr. Charlie is
selling. He sets them down at the foot of the bed as Mr. Charlie fishes in his
pocket for a quarter.*

MR. CHARLIE *(handing the coin to the Negro)*     Hyunh!
NEGRO *(breathlessly)*     Thankyseh!
30  MR. CHARLIE     Huh! You're too old a darkey to tote them big heavy cases.

NEGRO *(grinning sadly)*  Don't say that, Mistuh Charlie.

MR. CHARLIE  I reckon you'll keep right at it until yuh drop some day.

NEGRO  That's right, Mistuh Charlie. *(Mr. Charlie fishes in his pocket for another quarter and tosses it to the Negro, who crouches and cackles as he receives it.)*

MR. CHARLIE  Hyunh!

NEGRO  Thankyseh, thankyseh!

MR. CHARLIE  Now set that fan in motion an' bring me in some ice-water by an' by!

10  NEGRO  De fan don' work, Mistuh Charlie.

MR. CHARLIE  Huh! Deterioration! Everything's going downhill around here lately!

NEGRO  Yes, suh, dat's de troof, Mistuh Charlie, ev'ything's goin' downhill.

15  MR. CHARLIE  Who all's registered here of my acquaintance? Any ole-timers in town?

NEGRO  Naw, suh, Mistuh Charlie.

MR. CHARLIE  "Naw-suh-Mistuh-Charlie" 's all I get any more! You mean to say I won't be able to scare up a poker-game?

20  NEGRO *(chuckling sadly)*  Mistuh Charlie, you's de bes' judge about dat!

MR. CHARLIE  Well, it's mighty slim pickin's these days. Ev'ry time I come in a town there's less of the old and more of the new and by God, nigguh, this new stand of cotton I see around the Delta's not worth pickin' off th' ground! Go down there an' tell that young fellow, Mr. Bob Harper, to

25  drop up here for a drink!

NEGRO *(withdrawing)*  Yes, suh.

MR. CHARLIE  It looks like otherwise I'd be playin' solitaire!

*(The Negro closes the door. Mr. Charlie crosses to the window and raises the blind. The evening is turning faintly blue. He sighs and opens his valise*
30  *to remove a quart of whisky and some decks of cards which he slaps down on the table. He pauses and clasps his hand over his chest.)*

MR. CHARLIE *(ominously to himself)*  Boom-boom-boom-boom-boom! Here comes th' parade! *(After some moments there comes a rap at the door.)*  Come awn in! *(Harper, a salesman of thirty-five, enters. He has*
35  *never known the "great days of the road" and there is no vestige of grandeur in his manner. He is lean and sallow and has a book of colored comics stuffed in his coat pocket.)*

HARPER  How is the ole war-horse?

MR. CHARLIE *(heartily)*  Migthy fine an' dandy! How's the young squirrel?

HARPER   Okay.

MR. CHARLIE   That's the right answer! Step on in an' pour you'self a drink! Cigar?

HARPER *(accepting both)*   Thanks, Charlie.

5 MR. CHARLIE *(staring at his back with distaste)*   Why do you carry them comic sheets around with yuh?

HARPER   Gives me a couple of laughs ev'ry once and a while.

MR. CHARLIE   Poverty of imagination! *(Harper laughs a little resentfully.)* You can't tell me there's any real amusement in them things. *(He pulls it*

10 *out of Harper's coat pocket.)* "Superman," "The Adventures of Tom Tyler!" Huh! None of it's half as fantastic as life itself! When you arrive at my age – which is seventy-eight – you have a perspective of time on earth that astounds you! Literally astounds you! Naw, you say it's not true, all of that couldn't have happened! And for what *reason?* Naw! You begin to

15 wonder. ... Well ... You're with Schultz and Werner?

HARPER   That's right, Charlie.

MR. CHARLIE   That concern's a comparatively new one.

HARPER   I don't know about that. They been in th' bus'ness fo' goin' on twenty-five years now, Charlie.

20 MR. CHARLIE   Infancy! Infancy! You heard this one, Bob? A child in its infancy don't have half as much fun as adults – in their adultery! *(He roars with laughter. Harper grins. Mr. Charlie falls silent abruptly. He would have appreciated a more profound response. He remembers the time when a joke of his would precipitate a tornado. He fills up Harper's*

25 *glass with whisky.)*

HARPER   Ain't you drinkin'?

MR. CHARLIE   Naw, suh. Quit!

HARPER   How come?

MR. CHARLIE   Stomach! Perforated!

30 HARPER   Ulcers? *(Mr. Charlie grunts. He bends with difficulty and heaves a sample case onto the bed.)*   I had ulcers once.

MR. CHARLIE   *Ev'ry* drinkin' man has ulcers once. Some *twice.*

HARPER   You've fallen off some, ain't you?

MR. CHARLIE *(opening the sample case)*   Twenty-seven pounds I lost since

35 August. *(Harper whistles. Mr. Charlie is fishing among his samples.)* Yay-*ep!* Twenty-seven pounds I lost since August. *(He pulls out an oxford which he regards disdainfully.)* Hmmm ... a waste of cow-hide! *(He throws it back in and continues fishing.)*   A man of my age an' constitution, Bob – he oughtn't to carry so much of that – adipose tissue!

40 It's – *(He straightens up, red in the face and puffing.)* – a terrible strain –

on the *heart!* Hand me that other sample – over yonder. I wan' t' show
you a little eyeful of queenly footwear in our new spring line! Some
people say that the Cosmopolitan's not abreast of the times! That is an
allegation which I deny and which I intend to disprove by the simple
5   display of one little calf-skin slipper! *(opening up the second case)*  Here
we are, Son! *(fishing among the samples)*  You knew ole "Marblehead"
Langner in Friar's Point, Mississippi.

HARPER   Ole "Marblehead" Langner? Sure.

MR. CHARLIE   They found him dead in his bath-tub a week ago Satiddy
10   night. *Here's* what I'm lookin' faw!

HARPER   "Marblehead"? Dead?

MR. CHARLIE   *Buried!* Had a Masonic funeral. I helped carry th' casket.
Bob, I want you t' look at this Cuban-heel, shawl-tongue, perforated toe,
calf-skin Misses' sport-oxford! *(He elevates it worshipfully.)*  I want you
15   to look at this shoe – and tell me what you think of it in plain language!
*(Harper whistles and bugs his eyes.)*  Ain't that a piece of *real* merchandise, you squirrel? Well, suh, I want you t' know –!

HARPER   Charlie, that certainly is a piece of merchandise there!

MR. CHARLIE   Bob, that piece of merchandise is only a small indication – of
20   what our spring line consists of! You don't have to pick up a piece of
merchandise like that – with I.S.C. branded on it! – and examine it with
the microscope t' find out if it's quality stuff as well as quality *looks!* This
ain't a shoe that Mrs. Jones of Hattiesburg, Mississippi, is going to throw
back in your face a couple or three weeks later because it come to pieces
25   like *card*-board in th' first *rain!* No, suh – I want you to know! We got
some pretty fast-movers in our spring line – I'm layin' my samples out
down there in th' lobby first thing in th' mornin' – I'll pack 'em up an' be
gone out of town by *noon* – But by the Almighty Jehovah I bet you I'll
have to *wire* the office to mail me a bunch of *brand*-new order-books at
30   my next stopping-*off* place, Bob! *Hot* cakes! *That's* what I'm sellin'! *(He
returns exhaustedly to the sample case and tosses the shoe back in, somewhat disheartened by Harper's vaguely benevolent contemplation of the
brass light-fixture. He remembers a time when people's attention could be
more securely riveted by talk. He slams the case shut and glances irritably
35   at Harper who is staring very sadly at the brown carpet.)*  Well, suh – *(He
pours a shot of whisky.)*  It was a mighty shocking piece of news I
received this afternoon.

HARPER *(blowing a smoke ring)*   What piece of news was that?

MR. CHARLIE   The news about ole Gus Hamma – one of the old war-horses
40   from *way* back, Bob. He and me an' this boy's daddy, C. C., used t' play

poker ev'ry time we hit town together in this here self-same room! Well, suh, I want you t' know –

HARPER *(screwing up his forehead)*  I think I heard about that. Didn't he have a stroke or something a few months ago?

5  MR. CHARLIE  He *did.* An' partly *recovered.*

HARPER  Yeah? Last I heard he had t' be fed with a spoon.

MR. CHARLIE *(quickly)*  He did an' he partly recovered! He's been goin' round, y'know, in one of them chairs with a 'lectric motor on it. Goes chug-chug-chuggin' along th' road with th' butt of a cigar in his mouth.

10  Well, suh, yestuddy in Blue Mountain, as I go out the Elks' Club door I pass him comin' in, bein' helped by th' nigguh – "Hello! Hiyuh, Gus!" That was at six-fifteen. Just half an hour later Carter Bowman stepped inside the hotel lobby where I was packin' up my sample cases an' give me the information that ole Gus Hamma had just now burnt himself to death

15  in the Elks' Club lounge!

HARPER *(involuntarily grinning)*  What uh yuh talkin' about?

MR. CHARLIE  Yes, suh, the ole war-horse had fallen asleep with that nickel cigar in his mouth – set his clothes on fire – and burnt himself right up like a piece of paper!

20  HARPER  I don't believe yuh!

MR. CHARLIE  Now, why on earth would I be lyin' to yuh about a thing like that? He burnt himself right up like a piece of paper!

HARPER  Well, ain't that a bitch of a way for a man to go?

MR. CHARLIE  *One* way – *another* way –!  *(gravely)*  Maybe you don't *know*

25  it – but all of us ole-timers, Bob, are disappearin' *fast!* We all gotta quit th' road one time or another. Me, I reckon I'm pretty nearly the last of th' Delta drummers!

HARPER *(restively squirming and glancing at his watch)*  The last – of th' Delta drummers! How long you been on th' road?

30  MR. CHARLIE  Fawty-six yeahs in Mahch!

HARPER  I don't believe yuh.

MR. CHARLIE  Why would I tell you a lie about something like that? No, suh, I want you t' know – I want you t' know – Hmmm. ... I lost a mighty good customer this week.

35  HARPER *(with total disinterest, adjusting the crotch of his trousers)*  How's that, Charlie?

MR. CHARLIE *(grimly)*  Ole Ben Summers – Friar's Point, Mississippi ... Fell over dead like a bolt of lightning had struck him just as he went to pour himself a drink at the Cotton Planters' Cotillion!

40  HARPER  Ain't that terrible, though! What was the trouble?

MR. CHARLIE   Mortality, that was the trouble! Some people think that
millions now living are never going to *die*. I don't think that – I think it's a
misapprehension not borne out by the facts! We go like flies when we
come to the end of the summer ... And who is going to prevent it? *(He*
5   *becomes depressed.)*   Who – is going – to prevent it! *(He nods gravely.)*
The road is changed. The shoe industry is changed. These times are –
revolution! *(He rises and moves to the window.)*   I don't like the way
that it looks. You can take it from me – the world that I used to know –
the world that this boy's father used t' know – the world we belonged to,
10   us old time war-horses! – is slipping and sliding away from under our
shoes. Who is going to prevent it? The ALL-LEATHER slogan don't sell
shoes any more. The stuff that a shoe's made of is not what's going to sell
it any more! No! STYLE! SMARTNESS! APPEARANCE! That's what
counts with the modern shoe-purchaser, Bob! But try an' tell your style
15   department that. Why, I remember the time when all I had to do was lay
out my samples down there in the lobby. Open up my order-book an'
write out orders until my fingers *ached!* A *sales*-talk was not *necessary*. A
store was a place where people sold merchandise and to sell merchandise
the retail-dealer had to obtain it from the wholesale manufacturer, Bob!
20   Where they get merchandise now I do not pretend to know. But it don't
look like they buy it from wholesale dealers! Out of the air – I guess it
materializes! Or maybe stores don't *sell* stuff any more! Maybe I'm living
in a world of illusion! I recognize that possibility, too!

HARPER *(casually, removing the comic paper from his pocket)*   Yep – yep.
25   You must have witnessed some changes.

MR. CHARLIE   Changes? A mild expression. Young man – I have witnessed – a REVOLUTION! *(Harper has opened his comic paper but
Mr. Charlie doesn't notice, for now his peroration is really addressed to
himself.)*   Yes, a *revolution!* The atmosphere that I *breathe* is not the
30   same! Ah, well – I'm an old war-horse. *(He opens his coat and lifts the
multiple golden chains from his vest. An amazing number of watches rise
into view. Softly, proudly he speaks.)*   Looky here, young fellow! You
ever seen a man with this many watches? How did I *acquire* this many
time-pieces? *(Harper has seen them before. He glances above the comic
35   sheet with affected amazement.)*   At every one of the annual sales conven-
tions of the Cosmopolitan Shoe Company in St. Louis a seventeen-jewel,
solid-gold, Swiss-movement Hamilton watch is presented to the ranking
salesman of the year! Fifteen of those watches have been awarded to me!
I think that represents something! I think that's *something* in the way of
40   achievement! ... Don't *you?*

HARPER   Yes, *siree!* You bet I *do,* Mistuh Charlie! *(He chuckles at a remark in the comic sheet. Mr. Charlie sticks out his lips with a grunt of disgust and snatches the comic sheet from the young man's hands.)*

MR. CHARLIE   Young man – I'm talkin' to *you,* I'm talkin' for your *benefit.*
5   And I expect the courtesy of your attention until I am through! I may be an old war-horse. I may have received – the last of my solid gold watches ... But just the same – good manners are still a part of the road's tradition. And part of the *South's* tradition. Only a young peckerwood would look at the comics when old Charlie Colton is talking.

10   HARPER *(taking another drink)* Excuse me, Charlie. I got a lot on my mind. I got some business to attend to directly.

MR. CHARLIE   And directly you shall attend to it! I just want you to know what I think of this new world of yours! I'm not one of those that go howling about a Communist being stuck in the White House now! I don't
15   say that Washington's been took over by Reds! I don't say all of the wealth of the country is in the hands of the Jews! I like the Jews and I'm a friend to the niggers! I *do* say *this* – however. .... The world I knew is gone – gone – gone with the wind! My pockets are full of watches which tell me that my time's just about over! *(A look of great trouble and*
20   *bewilderment appears on his massive face. The rather noble tone of his speech slackens into a senile complaint.)* All of them – pigs that was slaughtered – carcasses dumped in the river! Farmers receivin' payment *not* t' grow wheat an' corn an' *not* t' plant cotton! All of these alphabet letters that's sprung up all about me! Meaning – unknown – to men of my
25   generation! The rudeness – the lack of respect – the newspapers full of strange items! The terrible – fast – dark – rush of events in the world! Toward what and where and why! ... I don't pretend to have any knowledge of now! I only say – and I say this very humbly – I don't understand – what's happened. ... I'm one of them monsters you see reproduced in
30   museums – out of the dark old ages – the giant *rep*-tiles, and the dino-whatever-you-call-ems. BUT – I *do* know *this!* And I state it without any shame! Initiative – self-reliance – independence of character! The old sterling qualities that distinguished one man from another – the clay from the potters – the potters from the clay – are *(kneading the air with his*
35   *hands)* How is it the old song goes? ... Gone with the roses of *yesterday!* Yes – with the *wind!*

HARPER *(whose boredom has increased by leaps and bounds)* You old-timers make one mistake. You only read one side of the vital statistics.

40   MR. CHARLIE *(stung)*   What do you mean by that?

HARPER   In the papers they print people *dead* in one corner and people *born* in the next and usually *one* just about levels *off* with the *other.*

MR. CHARLIE   Thank you for that information. I happen to be the god-father of several new infants in various points on the road. However, I
5   think you have missed the whole point of what I was saying.

HARPER   I don't think so, Mr. Charlie.

MR. CHARLIE   Oh, yes, you have, young fellow. My point is this: the ALL-LEATHER slogan is not what sells any more – not in shoes and not in humanity, neither! The emphasis isn't on quality. Production, produc-
10   tion, yes! But out of inferior goods! *Ersatz* – that's what they're making 'em out of!

HARPER *(getting up)*   That's your opinion because you belong to the past.

MR. CHARLIE *(furiously)*   A piece of impertinence, young man! I expect to be accorded a certain amount of respect by whippersnappers like
15   you!

HARPER   Hold on, Charlie.

MR. CHARLIE   I belong to – tradition. I am a *legend.* Known from one end of the Delta to the other. From the Peabody hotel in Memphis to Cat-Fish Row in Vicksburg. Mistuh Charlie – *Mistuh Charlie!* Who knows
20   *you?* What do *you* represent? A line of goods of doubtful value, some kike concern in the East! Get out of my room! I'd rather play solitaire, than poker with men who're no more solid characters than the jacks in the deck! *(He opens the door for the young salesman who shrugs and steps out with alacrity. Then he slams the door shut and breathes heavily.*
25   *The Negro enters with a pitcher of ice water.)*

NEGRO *(grinning)*   What you shoutin' about, Mistuh Charlie?

MR. CHARLIE   I lose my patience sometimes. Nigger –

NEGRO   Yes, suh?

MR. CHARLIE   You remember the way it used to be.

30   NEGRO *(gently)*   Yes, suh.

MR. CHARLIE   I used to come in town like a conquering hero! Why, my God, nigger – they all but laid red carpets at my feet! Isn't that so?

NEGRO   That's so, Mistuh Charlie.

MR. CHARLIE   This room was like a *throne*-room. My samples laid out over
35   there on green velvet cloth! The ceiling-fan *going* – now *broken!* And over here – the wash-bowl an' pitcher removed and the table-top *loaded* with *liquor!* In and out from the time I arrived till the time I left, the men of the road who knew me, to whom I stood for things commanding respect! Poker – continuous! Shouting, laughing – hilarity! Where have
40   they all gone to?

NEGRO *(solemnly nodding)* The graveyard is crowded with folks we knew, Mistuh Charlie. It's mighty late in the day!

MR. CHARLIE Huh! *(He crosses to the window.)* Nigguh, it ain't even late in the day any more – *(He throws up the blind.)* It's NIGHT! *(The space of the window is black.)*

NEGRO *(softly, with a wise old smile)* Yes, suh ... *Night*, Mistuh Charlie!

*Curtain*

## Biographical Notes

*Tennessee Williams was one of America's greatest dramatists, having influenced with his many plays not only the theater of his own country, but the international stage as well. Tennessee Williams was not so much a writer of the intellect as he was a dramatist of the emotions. He managed to evoke feeling and mood in his plays with great understanding.*

*Not surprisingly for a man who declared that writing was his reason for living, elements of Williams' private life found their way into his artistic creations. Born in Mississippi in 1911 to a very religious mother and a materialistic father, Williams grew up with contradictory impulses in his soul. They later manifested themselves in his writing.*

*After studying at various universities he wandered for several years, experiencing life at the lower realms of society. We see in his writing a remarkable sympathy for the misfit, the outcast, the down-and-out. They are portrayed as being caught in an unfriendly and hostile world.*

*"The Last of My Solid Gold Watches" comes from a volume of one-act plays published in 1946. His most famous plays, which were met with critical acclaim and financial success, are "The Glass Menagerie" (1945), "A Streetcar Named Desire" (1947) and "Cat on a Hot Tin Roof" (1955).*

*Suffering acutely in the 1960s from personal problems and a dependency on alcohol and pills, Williams experienced a psychological breakdown in 1969 and had to be institutionalized. But he continued to write plays. Tennessee Williams died in 1983.*

## Annotations

**43**  9 **deterioration** [dɪˌtɪərɪəˈreɪʃn] worsening of quality – 10 **blind** a window-shade – 11 **counterpane** cloth cover for a bed – 12 **pitcher** large jug – 13 **blindfolded** with a cover over the eyes – **lyre** [ˈlaɪə] harp-like instrument used by the ancient Greeks – 15 **lavish** [ˈlævɪʃ] having a lot of – 16 **superbly** [sjuːˈpɜːblɪ] **massive** *here:* noble, lordly, majestic – **bearing** behaviour and appearance – 17 **tidal** [ˈtaɪdəl] like an ocean wave – **puffs and rumbles** breathes quickly and makes a deep sound – 18 **to clasp** to hold tightly – **to cock** to turn, indicating attention – 19 **expanse** wide area – **to crisscross** to mark with lines which cross one another – 20 **fob** ornament attached to a watch chain – **trinket** [ˈtrɪŋkɪt] ornament or jewel of little value – 21 **suspended** hanging – **derby** *(A.E.)* bowler hat – 23 **drummer** *(chiefly A.E.)* s.o. who travels about selling goods – 24 **grizzled** grey-haired – **to tote** [təʊt] *(coll.)* to carry – 27 **a quarter** a twenty-five-cent coin – 28 **hyunh!** = here you are (one of several attempts to represent the way people actually speak) – 29 **thanky-seh!** = thank you, sir! – 30 **darkey** *(coll.)* black man (not polite)

**44**  2 **to reckon** *here:* to be of the opinion that – **to drop** *short for:* to drop dead – 4 **to crouch** [kraʊtʃ] to bend down – **to cackle** to laugh noisily, like a hen – 8 **by an' by** later on – 10 **de fan don' work** *(the porter's speech imitates the Southern black dialect)* = the fan does not work – 13 **dat's de troof** = that's the truth – 19 **to scare up** *here:* to cause to happen – 20 **to chuckle** to laugh gently – 21 **it's mighty slim pickin's** *(coll.)* there isn't much to choose from – 23 **stand** *here:* growth of plants – 26 **to withdraw** to leave – 27 **solitaire** [ˈsɒlɪteə] card-game for one player – 29 **valise** [vəˈliːz] *(A.E.)* small leather bag – 30 **deck** *here:* set – 32 **ominously** [ˈɒmɪnəslɪ] in a manner indicating s.th. bad is about to happen – 33 **rap** knock – 35 **vestige** [ˈvestɪdʒ] trace or sign – 36 **lean and sallow** thin and with an unhealthy yellow color – 39 **fine and dandy!** *(coll.)* very good

**45**  5 **distaste** dislike, aversion – 8 **resentfully** not liking s.th. – 13 **to astound** to overwhelm with surprise – 18 **for going on** *(coll.)* for about – 21 **adultery** *Ehebruch* – 22 **he would have appreciated** he would have liked – 23 **more profound** *here:* stronger – 24 **to precipitate a tornado** *here:* to result in a storm (of laughter) – 30 **ulcer** open sore usually in the stomach – **to grunt** to make a sound in an unclear manner – **to heave** to lift with difficulty – 37 **oxford** low shoe – 39 **adipose** [ˈædɪpəʊs] fatty

**46**  1 **over yonder** *(coll.)* over there – 3 **to be abreast of the times** to keep up with the times – 4 **allegation** charge, accusation – 12 **Masonic** [məˈsɒnɪk] from Mason or Freemason: a member of a secret all-male society – **casket** box in which one is buried – 13 **Cuban-heel** (... indicates fancy shoes) –

14 **elevates it worshipfully** lifts it up with great respect – 16 **bugs his eyes** opens his eyes very wide – **merchandise** ['mɜːtʃəndaɪz] s.th. to be sold – 21 **branded** printed – 25 **cardboard** very heavy paper – 30 **hot cakes** (from the expression, "selling like hot cakes": selling extremely well) – 31 **exhausted** very tired – **to toss** to throw – 32 **disheartened** discouraged – **vaguely benevolent** ... [bɪ'nevələnt] (Harper is stupidly absorbed in an object, wholly unaware of Charlie) – 34 **riveted** ['rɪvɪtɪd] strongly held – **glances irritably** ['– – – –] looks in an annoyed way

7   3 **to screw up one's forehead** to frown – 9 **butt** end – 10 **the Elks** fraternal organization that supports various charities – 16 **involuntarily** done without intention – 17 **nickel** five-cent coin; costing five cents – 23 **ain't that a bitch ...?** *(sl.)* isn't that a terrible way to die? – 24 **gravely** seriously – 28 **restively squirming** ['skwɜːmɪŋ] impatiently moving about – 35 **crotch** the place between a person's legs – 37 **grimly** sternly, seriously – 39 **cotillion** [kə'tɪljən] a formal ball

8   1 **mortality** *Sterblichkeit* – 3 **misapprehension** incorrect idea which is not proved by fact – 5 **grave** earnest, solemn – 19 **retail dealer ... wholesale manufacturer** *Einzelhändler ... Großhändler, Hersteller* – 24 **casually** ['kæʒjʊəlɪ] in a careless way – 25 **to witness** to see – 28 **peroration** [ˌperə'reɪʃn] *here:* lengthy speech – 34 **timepiece** watch, clock – 35 **affected** pretended, not genuine – 37 **ranking** of highest rank, e.g. most successful

9   3 **disgust** strong disapproval – 4 **benefit** good – 5 **courtesy** ['kɜːtɪsɪ] politeness – 8 **peckerwood** poor Southern white person – 14 **Communist ... in the White House** opponents of Franklin D. Roosevelt (American president 1933–45) accused him of being a communist – 20 **bewilderment** state of being confused – 21 **to slacken** to become slower, less active – 22 **to slaughter** ['slɔːtə] to kill – **carcass** ['kɑːkəs] dead body of an animal – 23 **alphabet letters** reference to the government agencies created by President Roosevelt to lead the country out of the depression; the agencies were referred to by abbreviations – 32 **self-reliance** confidence in one's own efforts – 33 **sterling** having the highest standard – **clay** a kind of earth – 34 **potter** person who makes articles out of clay – **to knead** [niːd] to work on material (flour, clay, etc.) with the hands – 37 **by leaps and bounds** immensely, quickly – 40 **to sting** *here:* to cause s.o. sharp pain with words

10   13 **furiously** angrily – **impertinence** *Unverschämtheit* – **to accord** to give – 14 **whippersnapper** a (young) person who is too bold and self-confident – 21 **kike** *(sl.)* Jew *(derogatory)* – 22 **jack** a playing card *(Bube)* – 23 **to shrug** to raise the shoulders in a manner indicating doubt, indifference – 24 **alacrity** [ə'lækrətɪ] cheerful willingness – 35 **velvet** *Samt* – 38 **to command** *here:* to deserve and get – 39 **hilarity** [hɪ'lærɪtɪ] loud laughter

## Edward Albee

# The Zoo Story

The Players:

PETER:

*A man in his early forties, neither fat nor gaunt, neither handsome nor homely. He wears tweeds, smokes a pipe, carries horn-rimmed glasses.*
5 *Although he is moving into middle age, his dress and his manner would suggest a man younger.*

JERRY:

*A man in his late thirties, not poorly dressed, but carelessly. What was once a trim and lightly muscled body has begun to go to fat; and while he is no*
10 *longer handsome, it is evident that he once was. His fall from physical grace should not suggest debauchery; he has, to come closest to it, a great weariness.*

The Scene:

*It is Central Park; a Sunday afternoon in summer; the present. There are*
15 *two park benches, one toward either side of the stage; they both face the audience. Behind them: foliage, trees, sky. At the beginning, Peter is seated on one of the benches.*

Stage Directions:

*As the curtain rises, Peter is seated on the bench stage-right. He is reading a*
20 *book. He stops reading, cleans his glasses, goes back to reading. Jerry enters.*

JERRY  I've been to the zoo. *(Peter doesn't notice)*  I said, I've been to the zoo. MISTER, I'VE BEEN TO THE ZOO!

PETER  Hm? ... What? ... I'm sorry, were you talking to me?

25 JERRY  I went to the zoo, and then I walked until I came here. Have I been walking north?

PETER *(puzzled)*  North? Why ... I ... I think so. Let me see.

JERRY *(pointing past the audience)*  Is that Fifth Avenue?

PETER  Why yes; yes, it is.

30 JERRY  And what is that cross street there; that one, to the right?

PETER  That? Oh, that's Seventy-fourth Street.

JERRY  And the zoo is around Sixty-fifth Street; so, I've been walking north.

PETER *(anxious to get back to his reading)*   Yes; it would seem so.

JERRY   Good old north.

PETER *(lightly, by reflex)*   Ha, ha.

JERRY *(after a slight pause)*   But not due north.

5  PETER   I ... well, no, not due north; but, we ... call it north. It's northerly.

JERRY *(watches as Peter, anxious to dismiss him, prepares his pipe)*   Well,
   boy; *you're* not going to get lung cancer, are you?

PETER *(looks up, a little annoyed, then smiles)*   No, sir. Not from this.

JERRY   No, sir. What you'll probably get is cancer of the mouth, and then

10   you'll have to wear one of those things Freud wore after they took one
   whole side of his jaw away. What do they call those things?

PETER *(uncomfortable)*   A prosthesis?

JERRY   The very thing! A prosthesis. You're an educated man, aren't you?
   Are you a doctor?

15  PETER   Oh, no; no. I read about it somewhere; *Time* magazine, I think.
   *(He turns to his book.)*

JERRY   Well, *Time* magazine isn't for blockheads.

PETER   No, I suppose not.

JERRY *(after a pause)*   Boy, I'm glad that's Fifth Avenue there.

20  PETER *(vaguely)*   Yes.

JERRY   I don't like the west side of the park much.

PETER   Oh? *(then, slightly wary, but interested)*   Why?

JERRY *(offhand)*   I don't know.

PETER   Oh. *(He returns to his book.)*

25  JERRY *(He stands for a few seconds, looking at Peter, who finally looks up
   again, puzzled.)*   Do you mind if we talk?

PETER *(obviously minding)*   Why ... no, no.

JERRY   Yes you do; you do.

PETER *(Puts his book down, his pipe out and away, smiling.)*   No, really; I

30   don't mind.

JERRY   Yes you do.

PETER *(finally decided)*   No; I don't mind at all, really.

JERRY   It's ... it's a nice day.

PETER *(stares unnecessarily at the sky)*   Yes. Yes, it is; lovely.

35  JERRY   I've been to the zoo.

PETER   Yes, I think you said so ... didn't you?

JERRY   You'll read about it in the papers tomorrow, if you don't see it on
   your TV tonight. You have TV, haven't you?

PETER   Why yes, we have two; one for the children.

40  JERRY   You're married!

PETER *(with pleased emphasis)*  Why, certainly.

JERRY  It isn't a law, for God's sake.

PETER  No ... no, of course not.

JERRY  And you have a wife.

5 PETER *(bewildered by the seeming lack of communication)*  Yes!

JERRY  And you have children.

PETER  Yes; two.

JERRY  Boys?

PETER  No, girls ... both girls.

10 JERRY  But you wanted boys.

PETER  Well ... naturally, every man wants a son, but ...

JERRY *(lightly mocking)*  But that's the way the cookie crumbles?

PETER *(annoyed)*  I wasn't going to say that.

JERRY  And you're not going to have any more kids, are you?

15 PETER *(a bit distantly)*  No. No more. *(then back, and irksome)*  Why did
you say that? How would you know about that?

JERRY  The way you cross your legs, perhaps; something in the voice. Or
maybe I'm just guessing. Is it your wife?

PETER *(furious)*  That's none of your business! *(a silence)*  Do you under-
20 stand? *(Jerry nods. Peter is quiet now.)*  Well, you're right. We'll have
no more children.

JERRY *(softly)*  That *is* the way the cookie crumbles.

PETER *(forgiving)*  Yes ... I guess so.

JERRY  Well, now; what else?

25 PETER  What were you saying about the zoo ... that I'd read about it, or
see ...?

JERRY  I'll tell you about it, soon. Do you mind if I ask you questions?

PETER  Oh, not really.

JERRY  I'll tell you why I do it; I don't talk to many people – except to say
30 like: give me a beer, or where's the john, or what time does the feature go
on, or keep your hands to yourself, buddy. You know – things like that.

PETER  I must say I don't ...

JERRY  But every once in a while I like to talk to somebody, really *talk;* like
to get to know somebody, know all about him.

35 PETER *(lightly laughing, still a little uncomfortable)*  And am I the guinea
pig for today?

JERRY  On a sun-drenched Sunday afternoon like this? Who better than a
nice married man with two daughters and ... uh ... a dog? *(Peter shakes
his head.)*  No? Two dogs. *(Peter shakes his head again.)*  Hm. No
40 dogs? *(Peter shakes his head, sadly.)*  Oh, that's a shame. But you look

like an animal man. CATS? *(Peter nods his head, ruefully.)* Cats! But,
that can't be your idea. No, sir. Your wife and daughters? *(Peter nods
his head.)* Is there anything else I should know?

PETER *(He has to clear his throat.)* There are ... there are two parakeets.
5   One ... uh ... one for each of my daughters.

JERRY   Birds.

PETER   My daughters keep them in a cage in their bedroom.

JERRY   Do they carry disease? The birds.

PETER   I don't believe so.

10 JERRY   That's too bad. If they did you could set them loose in the house and
the cats could eat them and die, maybe. *(Peter looks blank for a
moment, then laughs.)* And what else? What do you do to support your
enormous household?

PETER   I ... uh ... I have an executive position with a ... a small publishing
15   house. We ... uh ... we publish textbooks.

JERRY   That sounds nice; very nice. What do you make?

PETER *(still cheerful)*   Now look here!

JERRY   Oh, come on.

PETER   Well, I make around eighteen thousand a year, but I don't carry
20   more than forty dollars at any one time ... in case you're a ... a holdup
man ... ha, ha, ha.

JERRY *(ignoring the above)*   Where do you live? *(Peter is reluctant.)* Oh,
look; I'm not going to rob you, and I'm not going to kidnap your parakeets, your cats, or your daughters.

25 PETER *(too loud)*   I live between Lexington and Third Avenue, on Seventy-
fourth Street.

JERRY   That wasn't so hard, was it?

PETER   I didn't mean to seem ... ah ... it's that you don't really carry on a
conversation; you just ask questions, and I'm ... I'm normally ... uh ...
30   reticent. Why do you just stand there?

JERRY   I'll start walking around in a little while, and eventually I'll sit
down. *(recalling)* Wait until you see the expression on his face.

PETER   What? Whose face? Look here; is this something about the zoo?

JERRY *(distantly)*   The what?

35 PETER   The zoo; the zoo. Something about the zoo.

JERRY   The zoo?

PETER   You've mentioned it several times.

JERRY *(still distant, but returning abruptly)*   The zoo? Oh, yes; the zoo. I
was there before I came here. I told you that. Say, what's the dividing line
40   between upper-middle-middle-class and lower-upper-middle-class?

PETER   My dear fellow, I ...

JERRY   Don't my dear fellow me.

PETER *(unhappily)*   Was I patronizing? I believe I was; I'm sorry. But, you
see, your question about the classes bewildered me.

5 JERRY   And when you're bewildered you become patronizing?

PETER   I ... I don't express myself too well, sometimes. *(He attempts a
joke on himself.)*   I'm in publishing, not writing.

JERRY *(amused, but not at the humor)*   So be it. The truth *is I* was being
patronizing.

10 PETER   Oh, now; you needn't say that.

*(It is at this point that Jerry may begin to move about the stage with slowly
increasing determination and authority, but pacing himself, so that the long
speech about the dog comes at the high point of the arc.)*

JERRY   All right. Who are your favorite writers? Baudelaire and J. P.
15   Marquand?

PETER *(Wary)*   Well, I like a great many writers; I have a considerable ...
catholicity of taste, if I may say so. Those two men are fine, each in his
way. *(warming up)*   Baudelaire, of course ... uh ... is by far the finer of
the two, but Marquand has a place ... in our ... uh ... national ...

20 JERRY   Skip it.

PETER   I ... sorry.

JERRY   Do you know what I did before I went to the zoo today? I walked all
the way up Fifth Avenue from Washington Square; all the way.

PETER   Oh; you live in the Village! *(This seems to enlighten Peter.)*

25 JERRY   No, I don't. I took the subway down to the Village so I could walk
all the way up Fifth Avenue to the zoo. It's one of those things a person
has to do; sometimes a person has to go a very long distance out of his
way to come back a short distance correctly.

PETER *(almost pouting)*   Oh, I thought you lived in the Village.

30 JERRY   What were you trying to do? Make sense out of things? Bring
order? The old pigeonhole bit? Well, that's easy; I'll tell you. I live in a
four-story brownstone rooming-house on the upper West Side between
Columbus Avenue and Central Park West. I live on the top floor; rear;
west. It's a laughably small room, and one of my walls is made of beaver-
35   board; this beaverboard separates my room from another laughably small
room, so I assume that the two rooms were once one room, a small room,
but not necessarily laughable. The room beyond my beaverboard wall is
occupied by a colored queen who always keeps his door open; well, not
always, but *always* when he's plucking his eyebrows, which he does with

Buddhist concentration. This colored queen has rotten teeth, which is rare, and he has a Japanese kimono, which is also pretty rare; and he wears this kimono to and from the john in the hall, which is pretty frequent. I mean, he goes to the john a lot. He never bothers me, and he
5 never brings anyone up to his room. All he does is pluck his eyebrows, wear his kimono and go to the john. Now, the two front rooms on my floor are a little larger, I guess; but they're pretty small, too. There's a Puerto Rican family in one of them, a husband, a wife, and some kids; I don't know how many. These people entertain a lot. And in the other
10 front room, there's somebody living there, but I don't know who it is. I've never seen who it is. Never. Never ever.

PETER *(embarrassed)* Why ... why do you live there?

JERRY *(from a distance again)* I don't know.

PETER It doesn't sound like a very nice place ... where you live.

15 JERRY Well, no; it isn't an apartment in the East Seventies. But, then again, I don't have one wife, two daughters, two cats and two parakeets. What I do have, I have toilet articles, a few clothes, a hot plate that I'm not supposed to have, a can opener, one that works with a key, you know; a knife, two forks, and two spoons, one small, one large; three
20 plates, a cup, a saucer, a drinking glass, two picture frames, both empty, eight or nine books, a pack of pornographic playing cards, regular deck, an old Western Union typewriter that prints nothing but capital letters, and a small strongbox without a lock which has in it ... what? Rocks! Some rocks ... sea-rounded rocks I picked up on the beach when I was a
25 kid. Under which ... weighed down ... are some letters ... please letters ... please why don't you do this, and please when will you do that letters. And when letters, too. When will you write? When will you come? When? These letters are from more recent years.

PETER *(stares glumly at his shoes, then)* About those two empty picture
30 frames ...?

JERRY I don't see why they need any explanation at all. Isn't it clear? I don't have pictures of anyone to put in them.

PETER Your parents ... perhaps ... a girl friend ...

JERRY You're a very sweet man, and you're possessed of a truly enviable
35 innocence. But good old Mom and good old Pop are dead ... you know? ... I'm broken up about it, too ... I mean really. BUT. That particular vaudeville act is playing the cloud circuit now, so I don't see how I can look at them, all neat and framed. Besides, or, rather, to be pointed about it, good old Mom walked out on good old Pop when I was ten and a
40 half years old; she embarked on an adulterous turn of our southern states

... a journey of a year's duration ... and her most constant companion
... among others, among many others ... was a Mr. Barleycorn. At least,
that's what good old Pop told me after he went down ... came back ...
brought her body north. We'd received the news between Christmas and
5   New Year's, you see, that good old Mom had parted with the ghost in
some dump in Alabama. And, without the ghost ... she was less welcome. I mean, what was she? A stiff ... a northern stiff. At any rate,
good old Pop celebrated the New Year for an even two weeks and then
slapped into the front of a somewhat moving city omnibus, which sort of
10   cleaned things out family-wise. Well no; then there was Mom's sister,
who was given neither to sin nor the consolations of the bottle. I moved
in on her, and my memory of her is slight excepting I remember still that
she did all things dourly: sleeping, eating, working, praying. She dropped
dead on the stairs to her apartment, my apartment then, too, on the
15   afternoon of my high school graduation. A terribly middle-European
joke, if you ask me.

PETER   Oh, my; oh, my.

JERRY   Oh, your what? But that was a long time ago, and I have no feeling
about any of it that I care to admit to myself. Perhaps you can see,
20   though, why good old Mom and good old Pop are frameless. What's your
name? Your first name?

PETER   I'm Peter.

JERRY   I'd forgotten to ask you. I'm Jerry.

PETER   *(with a slight, nervous laugh)*   Hello, Jerry.

25   JERRY   *(nods his hello)*   And let's see now; what's the point of having a girl's
picture, especially in two frames? I have two picture frames, you
remember. I never see the pretty little ladies more than once, and most of
them wouldn't be caught in the same room with a camera. It's odd, and I
wonder if it's sad.

30   PETER   The girls?

JERRY   No. I wonder if it's sad that I never see the little ladies more than
once. I've never been able to have sex with, or, how is it put? ... make
love to anybody more than once. Once; that's it. ... Oh, wait; for a week
and a half, when I was fifteen ... and I hang my head in shame that
35   puberty was late ... I was a h-o-m-o-s-e-x-u-a-l. I mean, I was queer ...
*(very fast)*   ... queer, queer, queer ... with bells ringing, banners snap-
ping in the wind. And for those eleven days, I met at least twice a day
with the park superindendent's son ... a Greek boy, whose birthday was
the same as mine, except that he was a year older. I think I was very much
40   in love ... maybe just with sex. But that was the jazz of a very special

hotel, wasn't it? And now; oh, do I love the little ladies; really, I love
them. For about an hour.

PETER   Well, it seems perfectly simple to me. ...

JERRY *(angry)*   Look! Are you going to tell me to get married and have
5   parakeets?

PETER *(angry himself)*   Forget the parakeets! And stay single if you want
to. It's no business of mine. I didn't start this conversation in the ...

JERRY   All right, all right. I'm sorry. All right? You're not angry?

PETER *(laughing)*   No, I'm not angry.

10  JERRY *(relieved)*   Good. *(Now back to his previous tone.)* Interesting that
you asked me about the picture frames. I would have thought that you
would have asked me about the pornographic playing cards.

PETER *(with a knowing smile)*   Oh, I've seen those cards.

JERRY   That's not the point. *(laughs)* I suppose when you were a kid you
15   and your pals passed them around, or you had a pack of your own.

PETER   Well, I guess a lot of us did.

JERRY   And you threw them away just before you got married.

PETER   Oh, now; look here. I didn't *need* anything like that when I got
older.

20  JERRY   No?

PETER *(embarrassed)*   I'd rather not talk about these things.

JERRY   So? Don't. Besides, I wasn't trying to plumb your post-adolescent
sexual life and hard times; what I wanted to get at is the value difference
between pornographic playing cards when you're a kid, and pornographic
25   playing cards when you're older. It's that when you're a kid you use the
cards as a substitute for a real experience, and when you're older you use
real experience as a substitute for the fantasy. But I imagine you'd rather
hear about what happened at the zoo.

PETER *(enthusiastic)*   Oh, yes; the zoo. *(then, awkward)* That is ... if
30   you. ...

JERRY   Let me tell you about why I went ... well, let me tell you some
things. I've told you about the fourth floor of the roominghouse where I
live. I think the rooms are better as you go down, floor by floor. I guess
they are; I don't know. I don't know any of the people on the third and
35   second floors. Oh, wait! I do know that there's a lady living on the third
floor, in the front. I know because she cries all the time. Whenever I go
out or come back in, whenever I pass her door, I always hear her crying,
muffled, but ... very determined. Very determined indeed. But the one
I'm getting to, and all about the dog, is the landlady. I don't like to use
40   words that are too harsh in describing people. I don't like to. But the

landlady is a fat, ugly, mean, stupid, unwashed, misanthropic, cheap, drunken bag of garbage. And you may have noticed that I very seldom use profanity, so I can't describe her as well as I might.

PETER   You describe her ... vividly.

5   JERRY   Well, thanks. Anyway, she has a dog, and I will tell you about the dog, and she and her dog are the gatekeepers of my dwelling. The woman is bad enough; she leans around in the entrance hall, spying to see that I don't bring in things or people, and when she's had her mid-afternoon pint of lemon-flavored gin she always stops me in the hall, and grabs
10   ahold of my coat or my arm, and she presses her disgusting body up against me to keep me in a corner so she can talk to me. The smell of her body and her breath ... you can't imagine it ... and somewhere, somewhere in the back of that pea-sized brain of hers, an organ developed just enough to let her eat, drink, and emit, she has some foul parody of sexual
15   desire. And I, Peter, I am the object of her sweaty lust.

PETER   That's disgusting. That's ... horrible.

JERRY   But I have found a way to keep her off. When she talks to me, when she presses herself to my body and mumbles about her room and how I should come there, I merely say: but, Love; wasn't yesterday enough for
20   you, and the day before? Then she puzzles, she makes slits of her tiny eyes, she sways a little, and then, Peter ... and it is at this moment that I think I might be doing some good in that tormented house ... a simple-minded smile begins to form on her unthinkable face, and she giggles and groans as she thinks about yesterday and the day before; as she believes
25   and relives what never happened. Then, she motions to that black monster of a dog she has, and she goes back to her room. And I am safe until our next meeting.

PETER   It's so ... unthinkable. I find it hard to believe that people such as that really *are*.

30   JERRY *(lightly mocking)*   It's for reading about, isn't it?

PETER *(seriously)*   Yes.

JERRY   And fact is better left to fiction. You're right, Peter. Well, what I have been meaning to tell you about is the dog; I shall, now.

PETER *(nervously)*   Oh yes; the dog.

35   JERRY   Don't go. You're not thinking of going, are you?

PETER   Well ... no, I don't think so.

JERRY *(as if to a child)*   Because after I tell you about the dog, do you know what then? Then ... then I'll tell you about what happened at the zoo.

40   PETER *(laughing faintly)*   You're ... you're full of stories, aren't you?

JERRY  You don't *have* to listen. Nobody is holding you here; remember
that. Keep that in your mind.

PETER *(irritably)* I know that.

JERRY  You do? Good. *(The following long speech, it seems to me, should*
5 *be done with a great deal of action, to achieve a hypnotic effect on Peter,*
*and on the audience, too. Some specific actions have been suggested, but*
*the director and the actor playing Jerry might best work it out for them-*
*selves.)* ALL RIGHT. *(As if reading from a huge billboard.)* THE
STORY OF JERRY AND THE DOG! *(Natural again.)* What I am
10 going to tell you has something to do with how sometimes it's necessary
to go a long distance out of the way in order to come back a short distance
correctly; or, maybe I only think that it has something to do with that.
But, it's why I went to the zoo today, and why I walked north ... northerly, rather ... until I came here. All right. The dog, I think I told you, is
15 a black monster of a beast: an oversized head, tiny, tiny ears, and eyes ...
bloodshot, infected, maybe; and a body you can see the ribs through the
skin. The dog is black, all black; all black except for the bloodshot eyes,
and ... yes ... and an open sore on its ... *right* forepaw; that is red, too.
And, oh yes; the poor monster, and I do believe it's an old dog ... it's
20 certainly a misused one ... almost always has an erection ... of sorts.
That's red, too. And ... what else? ... oh, yes; there's a gray-yellow-
white color, too, when he bares his fangs. Like this: Grrrrrr! Which is
what he did when he saw me for the first time ... the day I moved in. I
worried about that animal the very first minute I met him. Now, animals
25 don't take to me like Saint Francis had birds hanging off him all the time.
What I mean is: animals are indifferent to me ... like people *(He smiles*
*slightly.)* ... most of the time. But this dog wasn't indifferent. From the
very beginning he'd snarl and then go for me, to get one of my legs. Not
like he was rabid, you know; he was sort of a stumbly dog, but he wasn't
30 half-assed, either. It was a good, stumbly run; but I always got away. He
got a piece of my trouser leg, look, you can see right here, where it's
mended; he got that the second day I lived there; but I kicked free and
got upstairs fast, so that was that. *(puzzles)* I still don't know to this day
how the other roomers manage it, but you know what I *think:* I think it
35 had only to do with me. Cozy. So. Anyway, this went on for over a week,
whenever I came in; but never when I went out. That's funny. Or, it *was*
funny. I could pack up and live in the street for all the dog cared. Well, I
thought about it up in my room one day, one of the times after I'd bolted
upstairs, and I made up my mind. I decided: First, I'll kill the dog with
40 kindness, and if that doesn't work ... I'll just kill him. *(Peter winces)*

Don't react, Peter; just listen. So, the next day I went out and bought a
bag of hamburgers, medium rare, no catsup, no onion; and on the way
home I threw away all the rolls and kept just the meat. *(Action for the
following, perhaps.)*   When I got back to the roominghouse the dog was
5 waiting for me. I half opened the door that led into the entrance hall, and
there he was; waiting for me. It figured. I went in, very cautiously, and I
had the hamburgers, you remember; I opened the bag, and I set the meat
down about twelve feet from where the dog was snarling at me. Like so!
He snarled; stopped snarling; sniffed; moved slowly; then faster; then
10 faster toward the meat. Well, when he got to it he stopped, and he looked
at me. I smiled; but tentatively, you understand. He turned his face
back to the hamburgers, smelled, sniffed some more, and then ...
RRRAAAAGGGGGHHHH, like that ... he tore into them. It was as if
he had never eaten anything in his life before, except like garbage. Which
15 might very well have been the truth. I don't think the landlady ever eats
anything but garbage. But. He ate all the hamburgers, almost all at once,
making sounds in his throat like a woman. *Then,* when he'd finished
the meat, the hamburger, and tried to eat the paper, too, he sat down
and smiled. I think he smiled; I know cats do. It was a very gratifying few
20 moments. Then, BAM, he snarled and made for me again. He didn't get
me this time, either. So, I got upstairs, and I lay down on my bed and
started to think about the dog again. To be truthful, I was offended, and I
was damn mad, too. It was six perfectly good hamburgers with not
enough pork in them to make it disgusting. I was offended. But, after a
25 while, I decided to try it for a few more days. If you think about it, this
dog had what amounted to an antipathy toward me; really. And, I won-
dered if I mightn't overcome this antipathy. So, I tried it for five more
days, but it was always the same: snarl, sniff; move; faster; stare; gobble;
RAAGGGHHH; smile; snarl; BAM. Well, now; by this time Columbus
30 Avenue was strewn with hamburger rolls and I was less offended than
disgusted. So, I decided to kill the dog. *(Peter raises a hand in protest.)*
Oh, don't be so alarmed, Peter; I didn't succeed. The day I tried to kill
the dog I bought only one hamburger and what I thought was a murder-
ous portion of rat poison. When I bought the hamburger I asked the man
35 not to bother with the roll, all I wanted was the meat. I expected some
reaction from him, like: we don't sell no hamburgers without rolls; or,
wha' d'ya wanna do, eat it out'a ya han's? But no; he smiled benignly,
wrapped up the hamburger in waxed paper, and said: A bite for ya pussy-
cat? I wanted to say: No, not really; it's part of a plan to poison a dog I
40 know. But, you can't say "a dog I know" without sounding funny; so I

said, a little too loud, I'm afraid, and too formally: YES, A BITE FOR
MY PUSSY-CAT. People looked up. It always happens when I try to
simplify things; people look up. But that's neither hither nor thither. So.
On my way back to the roominghouse, I kneaded the hamburger and the
rat poison together between my hands, at that point feeling as much
sadness as disgust. I opened the door to the entrance hall, and there the
monster was, waiting to take the offering and then jump me. Poor bastard; he never learned that the moment he took to smile before he went
for me gave me time enough to get out of range. BUT, there he was;
malevolence with an erection, waiting. I put the poison patty down,
moved toward the stairs and watched. The poor animal gobbled the food
down as usual, smiled, which made me almost sick, and then, BAM. But,
I sprinted up the stairs, as usual, and the dog didn't get me, as usual.
AND IT CAME TO PASS THAT THE BEAST WAS DEATHLY ILL.
I knew this because he no longer attended me, and because the landlady
sobered up. She stopped me in the hall the same evening of the attempted
murder and confided the information that God had struck her puppy-dog
a surely fatal blow. She had forgotten her bewildered lust, and her eyes
were wide open for the first time. They looked like the dog's eyes. She
sniveled and implored me to pray for the animal. I wanted to say to her:
Madam, I have myself to pray for, the colored queen, the Puerto Rican
family, the person in the front room whom I've never seen, the woman
who cries deliberately behind her closed door, and the rest of the people
in all roominghouses, everywhere; besides, Madam, I don't understand
how to pray. But ... to simplify things ... I told her I would pray. She
looked up. She said that I was a liar, and that I probably wanted the dog
to die. I told her, and there was so much truth here, that I didn't want the
dog to die. I didn't, and not just because I'd poisoned him. I'm afraid that
I must tell you I wanted the dog to live so that I could see what our new
relationship might come to. *(Peter indicates his increasing displeasure
and slowly growing antagonism.)* Please understand, Peter; that sort of
thing is important. You must believe me; it *is* important. We have to
know the effect of our actions. *(Another deep sigh.)* Well, anyway; the
dog recovered. I have no idea why, unless he was a descendant of the
puppy that guarded the gates of hell or some such resort. I'm not up on
my mythology. *(He pronounces the word myth-o-logy.)* Are you?
*(Peter sets to thinking, but Jerry goes on.)* At any rate, you've missed the
eight-thousand-dollar question, Peter; at any rate, the dog recovered his
health and the landlady recovered her thirst, in no way altered by the
bow-wow's deliverance. When I came home from a movie that was play-

ing on Forty-second Street, a movie I'd seen, or one that was very much like one or several I'd seen, after the landlady told me puppykins was better, I was so hoping for the dog to be waiting for me. I was ... well, how would you put it ... enticed? ... fascinated? ... no, I don't think so ... heart-shatteringly anxious, that's it; I was heart-shatteringly anxious to confront my friend again. *(Peter reacts scoffingly.)* Yes, Peter; friend. That's the only word for it. I was heart-shatteringly et cetera to confront my doggy friend again. I came in the door and advanced, un-afraid, to the center of the entrance hall. The beast was there ... looking at me. And, you know, he looked better for his scrape with the never-mind. I stopped; I looked at him; he looked at me. I think ... I think we stayed a long time that way ... still, stone-statue ... just looking at one another. I looked more into his face than he looked into mine. I mean, I can concentrate longer at looking into a dog's face than a dog can concen-trate at looking into mine, or into anybody else's face, for that matter. But during that twenty seconds or two hours that we looked into each other's face, we made contact. Now, here is what I had wanted to happen: I loved the dog now, and I wanted him to love me. I had tried to love, and I had tried to kill, and both had been unsuccessful by them-selves. I hoped ... and I don't really know why I expected the dog to understand anything, much less my motivations ... I hoped that the dog would understand. *(Peter seems to be hypnotized.)* It's just ... it's just that ... *(Jerry is abnormally tense, now.)* ... it's just that if you can't deal with people, you have to make a start somewhere. WITH ANIMALS! *(Much faster now, and like a conspirator.)* Don't you see? A person has to have some way of dealing with SOMETHING. If not with people ... if not with people ... SOMETHING. With a bed, with a cockroach, with a mirror ... no, that's too hard, that's one of the last steps. With a cock-roach, with a ... with a ... with a carpet, a roll of toilet paper ... no, not that, either ... that's a mirror, too; always check bleeding. You see how hard it is to find things? With a street corner, and too many lights, all colors reflecting on the oily-wet streets ... with a wisp of smoke, a wisp ... of smoke ... with ... with pornographic playing cards, with a strong-box ... WITHOUT A LOCK ... with love, with vomiting, with crying, with fury because the pretty little ladies aren't pretty little ladies, with making money with your body which is an act of love and I could prove it, with howling because you're alive; with God. How about that? WITH GOD WHO IS A COLORED QUEEN WHO WEARS A KIMONO AND PLUCKS HIS EYEBROWS, WHO IS A WOMAN WHO CRIES WITH DETERMINATION BEHIND HER CLOSED DOOR ...with

God who, I'm told, turned his back on the whole thing some time ago ...
with ... some day, with people. *(Jerry sighs the next word heavily.)*
People. With an idea; a concept. And where better, where ever better in
this humiliating excuse for a jail, where better to communicate one
5 single, simple-minded idea than in an entrance hall? Where? It would be
A START! Where better to make a beginning ... to understand and just
possibly be understood ... a beginning of an understanding, than with ...
*(Here Jerry seems to fall into almost grotesque fatigue.)* ... than with A
DOG. Just that; a dog. *(Here there is a silence that might be prolonged*
10 *for a moment or so; then Jerry wearily finishes his story.)* A dog. It
seemed like a perfectly sensible idea. Man is a dog's best friend,
remember. So: the dog and I looked at each other. I longer than the dog.
And what I saw then has been the same ever since. Whenever the dog
and I see each other we both stop where we are. We regard each other
15 with a mixture of sadness and suspicion, and then we feign indifference.
We walk past each other safely; we have an understanding. It's very sad,
but you'll have to admit that it is an understanding. We had made many
attempts at contact, and we had failed. The dog has returned to garbage,
and I to solitary but free passage. I have not returned. I mean to say, I
20 have *gained* solitary free passage, if that much further loss can be said to
be gain. I have learned that neither kindness nor cruelty by themselves,
independent of each other, creates any effect beyond themselves; and I
have learned that the two combined, together, at the same time, are the
teaching emotion. And what is gained is loss. And what has been the
25 result: the dog and I have attained a compromise; more of a bargain,
really. We neither love nor hurt because we do not try to reach each
other. And, *was* trying to feed the dog an act of love? And, perhaps, was
the dog's attempt to bite me *not* an act of love? If we can so misunder-
stand, well then, why have we invented the word love in the first place?
30 *(There is silence. Jerry moves to Peter's bench and sits down beside him.*
*This is the first time Jerry has sat down during the play.)* The Story of
Jerry and the Dog: the end. *(Peter is silent.)* Well, Peter? *(Jerry is*
*suddenly cheerful.)* Well, Peter? Do you think I could sell that story to
the *Reader's Digest* and make a couple of hundred bucks for *The Most*
35 *Unforgettable Character I've Ever Met?* Huh? *(Jerry is animated, but*
*Peter is disturbed.)* Oh, come on now, Peter; tell me what you think.

PETER *(numb)*  I ... I don't understand what ... I don't think I ... *(Now,*
*almost tearfully.)*  Why did you tell me all of this?

JERRY  Why not?

40 PETER  I DON'T UNDERSTAND!

JERRY *(furious, but whispering)*   That's a lie.

PETER   No. No, it's not.

JERRY *(quietly)*   I tried to explain it to you as I went along. I went slowly; it all has to do with ...

5   PETER   I DONT WANT TO HEAR ANY MORE. I don't understand you, or your landlady, or her dog. ...

JERRY   *Her* dog! I thought it was my ... No. No, you're right. It *is* her dog. *(Looks at Peter intently, shaking his head.)*   I don't know what I was thinking about; of course you don't understand. *(In a monotone, wear-*

10   *ily.)*   I don't live in your block; I'm not married to two parakeets, or whatever your setup is. I am a *permanent transient,* and my home is the sickening roominghouses on the West Side of New York City, which is the greatest city in the world. Amen.

PETER   I'm ... I'm sorry; I didn't mean to ...

15   JERRY   Forget it. I suppose you don't quite know what to make of me, eh?

PETER *(a joke)*   We get all kinds in publishing. *(Chuckles)*

JERRY   You're a funny man. *(He forces a laugh.)*   You know that? You're a very ... a richly comic person.

PETER *(modestly, but amused)*   Oh, now, not really. *(Still chuckling)*

20   JERRY   Peter, do I annoy you, or confuse you?

PETER *(lightly)*   Well, I must confess that this wasn't the kind of afternoon I'd anticipated.

JERRY   You mean, I'm not the gentleman you were expecting.

PETER   I wasn't expecting anybody.

25   JERRY   No, I don't imagine you were. But I'm here, and I'm not leaving.

PETER *(consulting his watch)*   Well, you may not be, but I must be getting home soon.

JERRY   Oh, come on; stay a while longer.

PETER   I really should get home; you see ...

30   JERRY *(tickles Peter's ribs with his fingers)*   Oh, come on.

PETER *(He is very ticklish; as Jerry continues to tickle him his voice becomes falsetto.)*   No, I ... OHHHHH! Don't do that. Stop, stop. Ohhh, no, no.

JERRY   Oh, come on.

35   PETER *(as Jerry tickles)*   Oh, hee, hee, hee. I must go. I ... hee, hee, hee. After all, stop, stop, hee, hee, hee, after all, the parakeets will be getting dinner ready soon. Hee, hee. And the cats are setting the table. Stop, stop, and, and ... *(Peter is beside himself now)*   ... and we're having ... hee, hee ... uh ... ho, ho, ho. *(Jerry stops tickling Peter, but the combi-*

40   *nation of the tickling and his own mad whimsy has Peter laughing almost*

    *hysterically. As his laughter continues, then subsides, Jerry watches him,*
    *with a curious fixed smile.)*

JERRY  Peter?

PETER  Oh, ha, ha, ha, ha, ha. What? What?

5 JERRY  Listen, now.

PETER  Oh, ho, ho. What ... what is it, Jerry? Oh, my.

JERRY *(mysteriously)*  Peter, do you want to know what happened at the
    zoo?

PETER  Ah, ha, ha. The what? Oh, yes; the zoo. Oh, ho, ho. Well, I had my
10    own zoo there for a moment with ... hee, hee, the parakeets getting
    dinner ready, and the ... ha, ha, whatever it was, the ...

JERRY *(calmly)*  Yes, that was very funny, Peter. I wouldn't have expected
    it. But do you want to hear about what happened at the zoo, or not?

PETER  Yes. Yes, by all means; tell me what happened at the zoo. Oh, my.
15    I don't know what happened to me.

JERRY  Now I'll let you in on what happened at the zoo; but first, I should
    tell you why I went to the zoo. I went to the zoo to find out more about
    the way people exist with animals, and the way animals exist with each
    other, and with people too. It probably wasn't a fair test, what with
20    everyone separated by bars from everyone else, the animals for the most
    part from each other, and always the people from the animals. But, if it's
    a zoo, that's the way it is. *(He pokes Peter on the arm.)*  Move over.

PETER *(friendly)*  I'm sorry, haven't you enough room? *(He shifts a little.)*

JERRY *(smiling slightly)*  Well, all the animals are there, and all the people
25    are there, and it's Sunday and all the children are there. *(He pokes Peter*
    *again.)*  Move over.

PETER *(patiently, still friendly)*  All right. *(He moves some more, and Jerry*
    *has all the room he might need.)*

JERRY  And it's a hot day, so all the stench is there, too, and all the balloon
30    sellers, and all the ice cream sellers, and all the seals are barking, and all
    the birds are screaming. *(Pokes Peter harder.)*  Move over!

PETER *(beginning to be annoyed)*  Look here, you have more than enough
    room! *(But he moves more, and is now fairly cramped at one end of the*
    *bench.)*

35 JERRY  And I am there, and it's feeding time at the lions' house, and the
    lion keeper comes into the lion cage, one of the lion cages, to feed one of
    the lions. *(Punches Peter on the arm, hard.)*  MOVE OVER!

PETER *(very annoyed)*  I can't move over any more, and stop hitting me.
    What's the matter with you?

40 JERRY  Do you want to hear the story? *(Punches Peter's arm again.)*

PETER *(flabbergasted)*  I'm not so sure! I certainly don't want to be punched in the arm.

JERRY *(punches Peter's arm again)*  Like that?

PETER  Stop it! What's the matter with you?

5 JERRY  I'm crazy, you bastard.

PETER  That isn't funny.

JERRY  Listen to me, Peter. I want this bench. You go sit on the bench over there, and if you're good I'll tell you the rest of the story.

PETER *(flustered)*  But ... whatever for? What *is* the matter with you?
10 Besides, I see no reason why I should give up this bench. I sit on this bench almost every Sunday afternoon, in good weather. It's secluded here; there's never anyone sitting here, so I have it all to myself.

JERRY *(softly)*  Get off this bench, Peter; I want it.

PETER *(almost whining)*  No.

15 JERRY  I said I want this bench, and I'm going to have it. Now get over there.

PETER  People can't have everything they want. You should know that; it's a rule; people can have some of the things they want, but they can't have everything.

20 JERRY *(laughs)*  Imbecile! You're slow-witted!

PETER  Stop that!

JERRY  You're a vegetable! Go lie down on the ground.

PETER *(intense)*  Now *you* listen to me. I've put up with you all afternoon.

JERRY  Not really.

25 PETER  LONG ENOUGH. I've put up with you long enough. I've listened to you because you seemed ... well, because I thought you wanted to talk to somebody.

JERRY  You put things well; economically, and, yet ... oh, what is the word I want to put justice to your ... JESUS, you make me sick ... get off here
30 and give me my bench.

PETER  MY BENCH!

JERRY *(pushes Peter almost, but not quite, off the bench)*  Get out of my sight.

PETER *(regaining his position)*  God da ... mn you. That's enough! I've had
35 enough of you. I will not give up this bench; you can't have it, and that's that. Now, go away. *(Jerry snorts but does not move.)* Go away, I said. *(Jerry does not move.)* Get away from here. If you don't move on ... you're a bum ... that's what you are. ... If you don't move on, I'll get a policeman here and make you go. *(Jerry laughs, stays.)* I warn you, I'll
40 call a policeman.

JERRY *(softly)*   You won't find a policeman around here; they're all over on the west side of the park chasing fairies down from trees or out of the bushes. That's all they do. That's their function. So scream your head off; it won't do you any good.

5 PETER   POLICE! I warn you, I'll have you arrested. POLICE! *(Pause)* I said POLICE! *(Pause)* I feel ridiculous.

JERRY   You look ridiculous: a grown man screaming for the police on a bright Sunday afternoon in the park with nobody harming you. If a policeman *did* fill his quota and come sludging over this way he'd prob-
10 ably take you in as a nut.

PETER *(with disgust and impotence)*   Great God, I just came here to read, and now you want me to give up the bench. You're mad.

JERRY   Hey, I got news for you, as they say. I'm on your precious bench, and you're never going to have it for yourself again.

15 PETER *(furious)*   Look, you; get off my bench. I don't care if it makes any sense or not. I want this bench to myself; I want you OFF IT!

JERRY *(mocking)*   Aw ... look who's mad.

PETER   GET OUT!

JERRY   No.

20 PETER   I WARN YOU!

JERRY   Do you know how ridiculous you look *now?*

PETER *(His fury and self-consciousness have possessed him.)*   It doesn't matter. *(He is almost crying.)*   GET AWAY FROM MY BENCH!

JERRY   Why? You have everything in the world you want; you've told me
25 about your home, and your family, and *your own* little zoo. You have everything, and now you want this bench. Are these the things men fight for? Tell me, Peter, is this bench, this iron and this wood, is this your honor? Is this the thing in the world you'd fight for? Can you think of anything more absurd?

30 PETER   Absurd? Look, I'm not going to talk to you about honor, or even try to explain it to you. Besides, it isn't a question of honor; but even if it were, you wouldn't understand.

JERRY *(contemptuously)*   You don't even know what you're saying, do you? This is probably the first time in your life you've had anything more trying
35 to face than changing your cat's toilet box. Stupid! Don't you have any idea, not even the slightest what other people *need?*

PETER   Oh, boy, listen to you; well, you don't need this bench. That's for sure.

JERRY   Yes; yes, I do.

40 PETER *(quivering)*   I've come here for years; I have hours of great pleasure,

great satisfaction, right here. And that's important to a man. I'm a
responsible person, and I'm a GROWNUP. This is my bench, and you
have no right to take it away from me.

JERRY  Fight for it, then. Defend yourself; defend your bench.

5 PETER  You've *pushed* me to it. Get up and fight.

JERRY  Like a man?

PETER *(still angry)*  Yes, like a man, if you insist on mocking me even
further.

JERRY  I'll have to give you credit for one thing; you *are* a vegetable, and a
10  slightly nearsighted one, I think ...

PETER  THAT'S ENOUGH. ...

JERRY  ... but, you know, as they say on TV all the time – you know – and I
mean this, Peter, you have a certain dignity; it surprises me. ...

PETER  STOP!

15 JERRY *(rises lazily)*  Very well, Peter, we'll battle for the bench, but we're not
evenly matched.  *(He takes out and clicks open an ugly-looking knife.)*

PETER *(suddenly awakening to the reality of the situation)*  You *are* mad!
You're stark raving mad! YOU'RE GOING TO KILL ME!  *(But before
Peter has time to think what to do, Jerry tosses the knife at Peter's feet.)*

20 JERRY  There you go. Pick it up. You have the knife and we'll be more
evenly matched.

PETER *(horrified)*  No!

JERRY *(rushes over to Peter, grabs him by the collar; Peter rises; their faces
almost touch)*  Now you pick up that knife and you fight with me. You
25  fight for your self-respect; you fight for that goddamned bench.

PETER *(struggling)*  No! Let ... let go of me! He ... Help!

JERRY *(slaps Peter on each "fight")*  You fight, you miserable bastard; fight
for that bench; fight for your parakeets; fight for your cats, fight for your
two daughters; fight for your wife; fight for your manhood, you pathetic
30  little vegetable. *(Spits in Peter's face.)*  You couldn't even get your wife
with a male child.

PETER *(breaks away, enraged)*  It's a matter of genetics, not manhood,
you ... you monster. *(He darts down, picks up the knife and backs off a
little; he is breathing heavily.)*  I'll give you one last chance; get out of
35  here and leave me alone! *(He holds the knife with a firm arm, but far in
front of him, not to attack, but to defend.)*

JERRY *(sighs heavily)*  So be it! *(With a rush he charges Peter and impales
himself on the knife. Tableau: For just a moment, complete silence, Jerry
impaled on the knife at the end of Peter's still firm arm. Then Peter
40  screams, pulls away, leaving the knife in Jerry. Jerry is motionless, on*

*point. Then he, too, screams, and it must be the sound of an infuriated and fatally wounded animal. With the knife in him, he stumbles back to the bench that Peter had vacated. He crumbles there; sitting, facing Peter, his eyes wide in agony, his mouth open.)*

5 PETER *(whispering)* Oh my God, oh my God, oh my God. ... *(He repeats these words many times, very rapidly.)*

JERRY *(Jerry is dying; but now his expression seems to change. His features relax, and while his voice varies, sometimes wrenched with pain, for the most part he seems removed from his dying. He smiles.)* Thank you,
10 Peter. I mean that, now; thank you very much. *(Peter's mouth drops open. He cannot move; he is transfixed.)* Oh, Peter, I was so afraid I'd drive you away. *(He laughs as best he can.)* You don't know how afraid I was you'd go away and leave me. And now I'll tell you what happened at the zoo. I think ... I think this is what happened at the zoo ... I think. I
15 think that while I was at the zoo I decided that I would walk north ... northerly, rather ... until I found you ... or somebody ... and I decided that I would talk to you ... I would tell you things ... and things that I would tell you would ... Well, here we are. You see? Here we *are*. But ... I don't know ... could I have planned all this? No ... no, I couldn't
20 have. But I think I did. And now I've told you what you wanted to know, haven't I? And now you know all about what happened at the zoo. And now you know what you'll see in your TV, and the face I told you about ... you remember ... the face I told you about ... my face, the face you see right now. Peter ... Peter? ... Peter ... thank you. I came unto you
25 *(He laughs, so faintly.)* and you have comforted me. Dear Peter.

PETER *(almost fainting)* Oh my God!

JERRY You'd better go now. Somebody might come by, and you don't want to be here when anyone comes.

PETER *(does not move, but begins to weep)* Oh my God, oh my God.

30 JERRY *(most faintly, now; he is very near death)* You won't be coming back here any more, Peter; you've been dispossessed. You've lost your bench, but you've defended your honor. And Peter, I'll tell you something now; you're not really a vegetable; it's all right, you're an animal. You're an animal, too. But you'd better hurry now, Peter. Hurry, you'd better go
35 ... see? *(Jerry takes a handkerchief and with great effort and pain wipes the knife handle clean of fingerprints.)* Hurry away, Peter. *(Peter begins to stagger away.)* Wait ... wait, Peter. Take your book ... book. Right here ... beside me ... on your bench ... my bench, rather. Come ... take your book. *(Peter starts for the book, but retreats.)* Hurry ... Peter.
40 *(Peter rushes to the bench, grabs the book, retreats.)* Very good, Peter ...

very good. Now ... hurry away. *(Peter hesitates for a moment, then flees, stage left.)* Hurry away. ... *(His eyes are closed now.)* Hurry away, your parakeets are making the dinner ... the cats ... are setting the table ...

5　PETER *(off stage)* *(A pitiful howl.)* OH MY GOD!

JERRY *(His eyes still closed, he shakes his head and speaks; a combination of scornful mimicry and supplication.)* Oh ... my ... God. *(He is dead.)*

*Curtain*

## Biographical Notes

*Edward Albee, one of America's most original playwrights, was adopted in 1928 when he was two weeks old by the wealthy owner of a chain of vaudeville theaters. His childhood seems to have been that of "The Poor Little Rich Boy". When he was twenty, he began a somewhat bohemian decade in Manhattan with the purpose of becoming a writer.*

*His New York years represent a difficult period in his life. It was at the height of despair over the course his life had taken that, in 1957, he sat down on the eve of his thirtieth birthday to type out "The Zoo Story" on a wobbly kitchen table.*

*With his "Zoo Story", Albee commanded attention; with "Who's Afraid of Virginia Woolf?" (first produced in 1962), he became famous.*

*Albee took the theater world by storm and was heralded as the American representative of the "Theater of the Absurd". Albee embraces this group's fundamental assertion that the human condition is essentially meaningless. "We do not have to live unless we wish to; the greatest sin in living is doing it badly ... stupidly, or as if you were not alive", he once declared. "All serious art", he has said, "is an attempt to modify and change people's perception of themselves, to bring them into larger contact with the fact of being alive." As for his method, he believes in provocation: "If the theater must bring us only what we can immediately apprehend or comfortably relate to, let us stop going to the theater entirely ..." He once said that people should come away from a performance "having suffered an experience of some sort ..."*

*His fame rests on "The Zoo Story" and "Who's Afraid of Virginia Woolf?" but Albee has written many other plays. "The Sandbox" (1959), "The American Dream" (1960), "Tiny Alice" (1965), "A Delicate Balance" (1966), "Box and Quotations from Chairman Mao Tse-Tung" (1969) and "All Over" (1971) are among the most important ones.*

**Annotations**

**54**  3 **gaunt** [gɔ:nt] lean, skinny – 4 **homely** not handsome; ugly – **horn-rimmed glasses** spectacles with frame made of material resembling (animal) horn – 9 **trim** in shape, fit – 10 **his fall from physical grace ...** the fact that he is no longer handsome – 11 **debauchery** [dɪ'bɔ:tʃərɪ] indulgence in sensual pleasures – 12 **weariness** tiredness, fatigue – 14 **Central Park** a large park in the center of Manhattan Island – 16 **foliage** ['fəʊlɪdʒ] leaves

**55**  4 **due** *adv.* directly, exactly – 6 **to dismiss** to send away – 11 **jaw** *Kiefer* – 12 **prosthesis** [prɒs'θi:sɪs] – 17 **blockhead** slow and stupid person – 22 **wary** ['weərɪ] careful, cautious – 23 **offhand** spontaneous, without thought

**56**  5 **bewildered** [bɪ'wɪldəd] puzzled, confused – 12 **that's the way the cookie crumbles** *(coll.)* there's nothing one can do – 15 **irksome** ['ɜ:ksəm] upset; annoyed – 19 **furious** extremely angry – 30 **john** *(sl.)* toilet – **feature** full-length film in a cinema program – 31 **buddy** *(sl.)* fellow – 35 **guinea pig** ['gɪnɪ] *Meerschweinchen; hier: Versuchskaninchen* – 37 **sun-drenched** soaked with sunshine

**57**  1 **ruefully** ['ru:fʊlɪ] pitifully, sadly, expressing regret – 4 **parakeet** *(A.E.)* budgerigar – 15 **textbook** book for use in school or university – 16 **what do you make?** *(informal)* how much do you earn? – 19 **eighteen thousand** (a considerable amount at the time the play was written) – 20 **holdup** robbery – 30 **reticent** ['retɪsənt] not saying much – 31 **eventually** finally, in the end – 32 **to recall** to bring back to the mind, to remember

**58**  3 **to patronize** ['pætrənaɪz] to treat s.o. as if he were an inferior person – 12 **to pace** to walk at a carefully determined step – 13 **arc** part of a circle – 17 **catholicity** [–-'–--] a wide range, a great number of things – 20 **skip it** *(coll.)* forget it – 24 **the Village** Greenwich Village, area of lower Manhattan where many artists live – **to enlighten** to make s.o. see clearly – 29 **to pout** [paʊt] *schmollen* – 31 **to pigeonhole** to put into (too) neat categories – **the old ... bit** *(coll.)* (a way of saying that s.th. is a common phenomenon) – 32 **brownstone** a typical building material of NYC houses – **rooming-house** *(A.E.)* a house where apartments and rooms are for rent – 34 **beaverboard** *Preßplatte* – 38 **queen** *(sl.)* a male homosexual who likes to appear as a female – 39 **to pluck** to pull out, usually one-by-one

**59**  1 **Buddhist concentration** total concentration – **rotten** decayed; having gone bad – 9 **to entertain** [ˌentə'teɪn] to have guests, visitors – 12 **(to be/feel) embarrassed** [ɪm'bærəst] to be ashamed, uneasy – 17 **hot plate** electric heater used to cook food – 21 **a deck** (of cards) a pack of playing cards – 23 **strongbox** *Geldkassette* – 29 **glum** gloomy, sad – 34 **enviable** ['envɪəbl] *beneidenswert* – 36 **to be broken up about s.th.** *(coll.)* to be extremely sad about s.th. – 37 **vaudeville** ['vɔ:dəvɪl] *(French)* a comic theatrical piece – **that particular ... is playing the cloud circuit** ['sɜ:kɪt] my parents are dead and in heaven (rather disrespectful) – 39 **to walk out on** to leave – 40 **to embark on** to engage in any enterprise – **adulterous turn** [ə'dʌltərəs] a tour/ trip involving sexual relationships with men other than her husband

**60** 2 **Mr. Barleycorn** = John Barleycorn *(coll.)*, whiskey (made from barley); an allusion to Jerry's mother being an alcoholic – 5 **to part with the ghost** to die – 6 **dump** *(sl.)* cheap, unattractive hotel or apartment house – **a stiff** *(sl.)* a dead body – 8 **for an even two weeks** for all of two weeks – 10 **family-wise** *(coll.)* in terms of the family – 11 **to be given to s.th.** to have as a habit – **consolation** comfort – 13 **dour** ['dʊə] severe; stern – 17 **oh, my** *(short for:)* oh, my goodness – 35 **queer** *(sl.)* homosexual – 38 **superintendent** *(A.E.)* person in charge of the upkeep of a building or, here, a park

**61** 15 **pal** *(coll.)* friend – 22 **to plumb** [plʌm] to get to the root of – **post-adolescent** [ˌædə'lesnt] when you're about to become an adult – 38 **muffled** indistinct – 40 **harsh** severe, cruel

**62** 1 **misanthropic** [ˌmɪsn'θrɒpɪk] hating or distrusting human society – 3 **profanity** [prə'fænɪtɪ] bad, vulgar language – 4 **vivid** clear, distinct – 6 **dwelling** ['dwelɪŋ] the place where s.o. lives – 14 **to emit** to give or send out – **foul parody** disgusting imitation – 21 **to sway** to move unsteadily, first to one side, then to the other – 22 **tormented** [tɔː'mentɪd] suffering – 24 **to groan** *stöhnen* – 40 **faint** weak; indistinct

**63** 3 **irritably** showing annoyance, anger – 8 **billboard** large advertisement sign, e.g. at the roadside – 16 **bloodshot** *blutunterlaufen* – 18 **paw** animal's foot – 22 **bares his fangs** shows his teeth – 28 **to snarl** to show the teeth and growl – **to go for s.o.** to attack – 29 **rabid** ['ræbɪd] affected with rabies *(Tollwut)*; mad – **stumbly** not walking with sureness – 30 **half-assed** *(sl.)* clumsy, imperfect – 35 **cozy** (usually said of a room) warm and comfortable – 38 **to bolt** [bəʊlt] to run away quickly – 40 **to wince** [wɪns] to make a facial gesture indicating mental pain or distress

**64** 2 **medium rare** not cooked completely – **catsup** ketchup – 6 **it figured** *(coll.)* that was to be expected – 11 **tentative** ['– – –] hesitant, careful – 19 **gratifying** satisfying, giving pleasure – 28 **to gobble** to eat fast, greedily, and noisily – 30 **to strew** to throw all over, to scatter – 37 **benign** [bɪ'naɪn] kind and gentle

**65** 3 **that's neither hither nor thither** *(coll.)* that's neither here nor there; that's irrelevant – 4 **to knead** [ni:d] to mix and shape with one's hands – 7 **poor bastard** (suggests pity mixed with hostility) – 9 **out of range** beyond reach – 10 **malevolence** [–'– – –] evil will – **patty** a round, flattened out piece of ground meat – 14 **it came to pass** highly formal, old-fashioned phrase (biblical language) – 16 **to sober up** ['səʊbə] to become serious; not be drunk any more – 17 **to confide s.th. to s.b.** [kən'faɪd] *anvertrauen* – 18 **fatal** ['feɪtl] deadly – 20 **to snivel** ['snɪvl] to complain in a miserable, whining way – **to implore** [ɪm'plɔ:] *anflehen* – 23 **deliberately** [dɪ'lɪbrətlɪ] (done) on purpose – 35 **resort** *(here iron.)* a popular place of entertainment or recreation (cf. a seaside resort) – **to be up on s.th.** *(coll.)* to be well-informed about s.th. – 40 **bow-wow** (baby talk) dog – **deliverance** rescue

**66** 4 **enticed** [ɪn'taɪst] tempted – 5 **heart-shatteringly** to an extreme degree – 6 **to scoff** to mock – 10 **scrape with the nevermind** *here:* encounter with death – 27 **cockroach** ['kɒkrəʊtʃ] *Kakerlake* – 32 **wisp** thin, twisted piece of s.th. – 34 **to vomit** *sich übergeben* – 35 **fury** anger

**67** 4 **to humiliate** [hju'mɪlɪeɪt] to cause s.o. to feel ashamed – **jail** prison – 8 **fatigue** [fə'ti:g] condition of being very tired – 15 **to feign** [feɪn] to pretend – 19 **solitary** lonely; without companions – 25 **to attain** [ə'teɪn] to reach, arrive at – 34 **buck** *(sl.)* dollar – 35 **animated** ['––––] lively – 37 **numb** [nʌm] without ability to feel or move

**68** 8 **intently** [ɪn'tentlɪ] eagerly; earnestly – 11 **setup** ['setʌp] *(coll.)* arrangement, constellation – **transient** ['trænzɪənt] *(as noun, A.E.)* person who is not settled, who comes and goes – 16 **to chuckle** to laugh with mouth closed – 20 **to annoy** [ə'nɔɪ] to cause inconvenience, to irritate – 22 **to anticipate** [–'–––] to expect – 26 **to consult** to ask for advice, to look for information – 30 **to tickle** *kitzeln* – 32 **falsetto** [fɔ:l'setəʊ] unnaturally high-pitched voice in men – 38 **to be beside o.s.** to be out of control – 40 **whimsy** odd humor

**69** 1 **to subside** to become less – 22 **to poke** [pəʊk] to push with a stick, one's finger etc. – 23 **to shift** to move – 29 **stench** extremely unpleasant smell – 30 **seal** [si:l] *Seehund* – 37 **to punch** to hit hard with the fist

**70** 1 **to flabbergast** ['flæbəgɑ:st] to astonish – 9 **to fluster** to make nervous or confused – 11 **secluded** [sɪ'klu:dɪd] hidden, isolated – 14 **to whine** to complain in long-drawn sounds (like a dog, a siren etc.) – 20 **imbecile** ['ɪmbɪsi:l] idiot – **slow-witted** mentally slow – 23 **to put up with s.o. or s.th.** to tolerate s.o. or s.th. – 36 **to snort** to force the air with violence through the nose; to laugh loudly – 38 **bum** person leading an unsteady life

**71** 2 **fairy** *here: (sl.)* homosexual – 9 **quota** ['kwəʊtə] *here:* number of arrests a policeman is supposed to make – **to sludge** *etwa: vorbeischlappen* – 10 **nut** *(sl.)* person who is crazy – 11 **impotence** lack of strength or power – 33 **contemptuous** [kən'temptʃʊəs] completely disrespectful; disdaining – 34 **trying** difficult, challenging – 40 **to quiver** ['kwɪvə] to shake with excitement

**2** 9 **to give s.o. credit for s.th.** *here:* to assure s.o. of s.th. – 16 **to be evenly matched** to do s.th. under the same conditions, with the same equipment –

18 **stark raving mad** absolutely crazy – 19 **to toss** to throw with a quick, light motion – 29 **pathetic** [pə'θetɪk] pitiful – 30 **to get** = beget; to father, make pregnant – 32 **enraged** extremely angry – 33 **to dart** to move rapidly – 37 **to impale** [ɪm'peɪl] to pierce with s.th. sharp – 38 **tableau** scene

**73** 3 **to vacate** ['veɪkeɪt] to quit, to leave – **to crumble** *here:* to collapse – 4 **agony** extreme pain – 7 **his features relax** his face becomes less tense – 8 **wrenched** [rentʃt] violently twisted – 11 **transfixed** [–'–] held fixed or motionless – 31 **to dispossess** [ˌdɪspə'zes] to put out of possession – 37 **to stagger** to walk unsteadily, as from weakness or drunkenness – 39 **to retreat** to move back

**74** 6 **scornful mimicry** disrespectful imitation – **supplication** [ˌsʌplɪ'keɪʃn] humble prayer, asking for mercy, help etc.